THE KENNET AND AVON WALK

Chertsey Bridge (Section 4)

THE KENNET AND AVON WALK

A Walker's Guide from
London to Bristol

by

Ray Quinlan

CICERONE PRESS
POLICE SQUARE, MILNTHORPE

TO MARY

who was with me all the way
(if sometimes only in spirit)

Photographs by the author
Cover : Canal near Greenham Lock, (Section 3)

CONTENTS

Queen Elizabeth II lock, Devizes

INTRODUCTION

On the 8th of August 1990, in the middle of half an hour of alarming news about Iraq's invasion of Kuwait, the BBC carried a small piece from one of its West Country reporters. In bright sunshine and amid huge crowds, the Queen had unveiled a plaque to declare the Kennet & Avon Canal officially re-opened. It was an incongruous and, perhaps, slightly frivolous news item given the circumstances but this made it all the more welcome. A great waterway had finally recovered from its temporary indisposition and, although not in full health, was well on the way to regaining its former vigour. It was once again possible to navigate all the way from London to Bristol.

That one of the great canals has been restored is good news for boater, naturalist, industrial archaeologist and walker alike. The canal is a splendid piece of water; rich in good scenery, wildlife, history, archaeology and simple peace and quiet. It makes excellent walking territory, having both the long term goal of joining the South's premier cities, as well as the pleasure and interest that the individual sections can provide. It is a long-distance path of constant and fascinating variation and a route that is available to everyone.

London to Bristol via the Kennet & Avon Canal

The Kennet & Avon navigational route from London to Bristol strikes through the heart of southern England. From the centre of the nation's capital, the Thames twists and turns through the south-western suburbs to reach royal Windsor. These are areas of sustained historical interest. Kew, Richmond, Hampton Court, Runnymede and Windsor itself, have all been closely linked with the country's past as well as its development. From Windsor, the path enters rural Berkshire to pass through the pleasant Thames-side towns of Marlow and Henley. Then at Reading, the route joins the Kennet & Avon Canal; eighty-six and a half miles of man-made navigation from its junction with the Thames to Hanham Mills near Bristol.

The character of the canal is very different to that of London's river. It's quieter and more intimate. As we walk along its well-marked towpath, we pass through the country towns of Newbury and Hungerford before entering the peaceful charm of Wiltshire. Here are some of the canal's greatest technical achievements: the oldest beam engines in operation at Crofton, the Bruce Tunnel and the magnificent flight of Caen Hill locks at Devizes. Yet, despite this flurry of early nineteenth century industry, the villages are unspoilt and delightful.

From the headquarters and museum of the Canal Trust at Devizes, the path continues to the splendid town of Bradford-on-Avon, a kind of mini-Bath with its stone buildings and rich character. The way between Bradford and Bath passes through some great scenery and presents some more of the canal's wonderful history: two fine aqueducts and the fascinating water-powered Claverton pumping station.

Bath has virtually everything to offer the visitor; from rich history to lively present. Here the canal joins the River Avon and we return to the broad meandering of a river in maturity. The path passes through some lush countryside and the towns of Saltford and Keynsham to reach the tidal Avon at Hanham before entering the outskirts of Bristol. From here, some 164 miles from Westminster, the route ends at Bristol's famous floating harbour. Walkers can, however, continue onwards along the Avon Gorge and under the Clifton Suspension Bridge to see the sea: a full 171 miles from central London.

An Historic Link

People have wanted to travel or transport their goods between London and Bristol since mediaeval times. In the early days, this would have been done either on foot or by packhorse along some pretty miserable and occasionally dangerous roads. There was no easy-riding M4 or Inter-City railway. It was a long way and to ship heavy or bulky goods directly was virtually impossible. So it all went the lengthy and hazardous sea route. This route, always irksome, was, in times of war, often really dangerous with pirates rampant.

Several schemes to join the Avon with the Thames were suggested during the Elizabethan era but nothing came of them.

Further schemes were suggested in the seventeenth century when it was proposed to make the Avon navigable to Malmesbury and then to connect it with the Thames at either Cricklade or Lechlade. With the restoration of the monarchy in 1660, no fewer than four bills were presented to Parliament for the purpose of making a navigable link between London and Bristol. None of them succeeded. However, progress was made on two local schemes.

In 1723, at the behest of many towns to the west of Reading, the River Kennet was made navigable as far as Newbury; a distance of eighteen and a half miles. By 1727, at the behest of a group of powerful local entrepreneurs, the River Avon was made navigable from Bristol to Bath; a distance of seventeen miles.

But it wasn't until nearly sixty years later that a group came together to try once again to forge the complete link. Charles Dundas, an MP from Kintbury, and some colleagues, held a meeting to propose an extension of the Kennet Navigation to Hungerford. The attendees weren't so unambitious and asked the committee, of the then titled Western Canal, to investigate the potential of linking the Avon Navigation with the Kennet.

The engineer John Rennie was employed to carry out a survey and, with his recommendations, a follow-up meeting in Marlborough in November 1790 resolved unanimously to proceed with the route. With the coming of what is now called 'canal mania', there was no problem finding enough subscribers and in April 1794, the Kennet & Avon Canal Act received Royal Assent for a fifty-five-mile-long canal to link Newbury and Bath.

Building the canal proved to be harder than expected for business, geological and constructional reasons. From the time the first sod was cut at Bradford-on-Avon in October 1794, it took over sixteen years to complete. The last section to be opened was the flight of twenty-nine locks that scaled Caen Hill on the western side of Devizes.

Over the next thirty years or so the canal was a modest success. It regularly returned profits and dividends to its shareholders and was constantly busy carrying loads along sections or even the entire length of the canal. The cost of shipping goods from London to Bristol was reduced by well over fifty per cent, with a typical journey time (with a horse-drawn boat) of ten days (the fifty-five miles from Newbury to Bath averaged three and a half days). Later, with the use of daily, high-speed 'fly' boats, the London-Bristol time was reduced to five days.

The commercial success of the canal did not last long. In 1841 Brunel's Great Western Railway started running its service from London to Bristol and from then on the nails were firmly slotted into the K&A's coffin. Almost immediately all the through traffic from one city to the other was lost to the railway. To compete, the company cut wages and made economies and was thereby able to reduce its tolls - but it made no difference. More railways were built; for example the line almost following the canal to Pewsey was opened in 1848. By 1850 trade on the K&A had dropped to such an extent that when the dividend was paid for the operating year 1849-50, it was clear that the company would not be able to repeat the payout in the following year. The end came in 1852. The GWR Act No. 1 allowed the railway company to take over the canal in its entirety.

Despite the various legal constraints on the company forcing it to keep the navigation open, the GWR paid no real attention to the canal which gradually fell into disrepair. By the time the railways were nationalised in 1948, the canal was only barely passable and nationalisation didn't improve matters. From its poor post-war state, it fell into complete dereliction; locks fell apart, whole sections dried out. Eventually the British Transport Commission submitted a closure act to parliament in 1952.

A bunch of enthusiasts formed the Canal Association to fight the closure act. They were successful and thus brought about the birth of the Kennet & Avon Canal Trust. It is the trust that has been the driving force in the revival of the K&A's fortunes over the last twenty-five to thirty years. From modest beginnings, the trust has worked hand in hand with the British Waterways Board and others to gradually bring life back into the canal. Their day was that 8th August 1990 when the Queen successfully broke through the thirty minutes of doom and gloom that was the six o'clock radio news. It is once again possible to navigate from the Thames Estuary to the Bristol Channel by way of the K&A Canal.

The Walk

One of the great features of the Kennet & Avon route from London to Bristol is that it can be as long or as short as you want it to be. There's no setting off grim-faced and laden knowing that you won't see the inside of a pub or a dry sleeping bag again for another three weeks. But there again, neither is it a matter of turning around the first corner to find yourself back at the car park. You can walk the entire length from London to Bristol or just walk the Kennet & Avon Canal or simply have the occasional outing at selected points along the route. Walks can be four miles or ninety-three miles or one hundred and sixty-four miles or even the full 171 miles. You can do it in one concentrated leap or one hundred tiny hops. It's entirely up to you.

On the other hand towpath walking cannot provide the exhilaration of a rugged mountain climb. There's not a Tryfan or even a Loughrigg en route. Life on towpath walks is more subtle than that and, perhaps contrarily, more accessible. All of the paths along the walk are easy to walk on. All of the sections pass through countryside but start and end at places served by public transport and which have shops and accommodation. A pub is never more than about three or four miles away.

The London-Bristol route is not an officially recognised long distance footpath but is suitably marked for most of its length. The Thames Walk (from London to the source near Cricklade) has been recognised as a national route and it should be completed shortly. The Kennet & Avon has towpath waymark signs from Reading through to Bath. The route from Bath to Bristol is part of the Avon Walkway but is poorly signposted and has some gaps.

Scope of This Book

This book primarily concerns itself with the navigation system that was owned and run by the Kennet & Avon Canal Company. The main text describes the ninety-two and a half miles between Reading and Bristol in detail so that walkers can ramble along either the entire length of the canal or along individual sections. This basic walk can be extended. At the Reading end, the walk can be taken a further seventy-one and a half miles to Westminster. At the Bristol end, the Avon Walkway continues a further seven miles to the sea at Avonmouth. By doing this, the basic walk can be extended to form the London-Bristol long-distance route.

There is sufficient information in this book for you to be able to complete the Thames or Avonmouth sections perfectly satisfactorily but this volume does not go into great detail for those parts of the walk.

The Thames Path is a unique and interesting long-distance route in its own right and is adequately covered by many excellent books. It would simply be pointless to replicate what is already widely available. The author recommends the Ramblers' Association's *The Thames Walk* which is both informative and easy to follow, as well as being good value. It is available at bookshops or from Ramblers' Association, 1/5 Wandsworth Road, London SW8 2XX.

If you wish to follow the full course of the River Avon, Roger Jones has published his own *Down the Bristol Avon* (Ex Libris Press). Although not describing the Avon as a long-distance walk, it provides information and descriptions of fourteen round walks in the area. It is available from bookshops.

Organising Your Walk

It doesn't matter where you begin, or where you end, but this book is organised from right to left: London to Bristol. It had to go one way and having walked in that direction it seems as good as any. It has the benefit of getting out of London early and leaving some of the best bits to the end.

But you don't have to do the entire walk in one go. This is truly a long-distance route that can easily be done in short-distance steps. The book is divided into ten to seventeen-mile-long sections with advice on how to use public transport to return to cars or accommodation left at the starting point. These sections can be loosely viewed as suitable for one day's walking. Within each section, half-length (morning or afternoon) routes are suggested which can either be used as circular trips or, in many cases, half-distance walks with return by public transport.

Walkers should generally plan for two to two and a half miles an hour, so that stops can be made for sightseeing and refreshment. Head-down speedsters can easily muster three miles an hour on many of the canal sections on good to firm going, even with the occasional stop. As anyone who walks with them will know, keen photographers and bird-watchers could take for ever. Allow plenty of time if having such sluggardly companions.

For walkers who wish to cover a greater distance each day, the following eight night plan is recommended:

Westminster-Hampton Court-Windsor-Henley-Woolhampton-Great Bedwyn- Devizes-Bath-Bristol.

This averages about twenty to twenty-one miles a day (maximum twenty-two, minimum seventeen) and can be easily reversed if you wish to walk Bristol-London. In good summer weather, this should be easily achievable for suitably fit, practised and resilient walkers. Woolhampton and Great Bedwyn are both short of accommodation but are on the BR Bedwyn-Reading line for return to more populated places (NB. Trains don't stop at either place on Sundays).

However you plan to do it, the whole route makes easy walking and is along officially designated towpaths or public rights of way. The biggest hazard is the weather and the hardest slope is a slippery bit downhill from Winter Hill near Marlow (one of the benefits of a towpath walk is the lack of 'up'). Some parts of the walk can be muddy, especially on the river (rather than the canal) sections. Of course, walking along a waterway can present a danger for very young children and parents should take care to make sure that their offspring are safe at all times. There are remarkably few lifebuoys around anywhere along the canal or rivers.

Public houses are well and conveniently sited all the way along the route and always in a place handy for lunch. In some areas, particularly in Wiltshire, shops may be fewer and further apart but should be frequent enough to stock up. Walkers may, however, still be advised to always carry something to eat and drink, together with the usual waterproofs and a small first aid kit.

This book includes maps of the relevant sections of the walk. It is, however, impossible to include much information about the surrounding villages and towns and you may wish to purchase the relevant OS Maps. The appropriate numbers are: 172 (Bristol/Bath), 173 (Swindon/Devizes), 174 (Newbury & Wantage), 175 (Reading & Windsor) & 176 (West London). Alternatively (or in addition) in the canal section, you might prefer to buy one of the maps specific to the navigation. The K&A Trust publishes an excellent and reasonably priced map that is widely available in shops near the canal or at the trust headquarters in Devizes. There are also two navigational charts published by Imray, Lawrie, Norie & Wilson Ltd (St. Ives, Cambs). One covers Avonmouth to All Cannings, and the other All Cannings to Reading. These are more expensive and are aimed more specifically at boat users. They are also available locally.

In using this book, route directions are written in normal type. Miscellaneous personal observations, irreverent (and sometimes irrelevant) comment and fascinating information on the things to be seen are printed in *italic*. This means that if you find yourself in the pouring rain you can skip the mind-expanding minutiae to get to the directions or, alternatively, whilst shivering in the down-market hostelry later, you can skip the plodding stuff to get to the meaty bits. The beauty about any walk is that it's all up to you.

Natural History

Most waterways are excellent wildlife oases and the Kennet & Avon is no exception. The variety of habitats that are part of the navigation or attached to it is impressive, and so the number of species recorded is equally amazing.

They tell me that 120 species of bird have been seen along the canal. My list only reached the mid-40s but I wasn't looking that hard. I will say that people who are allergic to coots shouldn't do the walk and that the average plodder should be able to see more spectacular things like herons and kingfishers without too much difficulty (even my blurred vision picked out about ten kingfishers between Reading and Bath). The Kennet Valley osier beds are good places for nightingale, and the many reed beds thereabouts support relatively large numbers of warblers and buntings.

The changing geology along the walk means an interesting and varied flora. The walk is also, naturally, rich in water-loving species like yellow flag and arrowhead. Butterbur, meadow-sweet and comfrey appear to be on virtually every bank. I won't mention the stinging nettles or the tatty looking and aptly named mugwort which are both similarly rather common. In my view, probably the most fascinating niche for plants is the downstream side of the lock gate, where many a plant seems to cling tenaciously to this most awkward of habitats.

Take a stroll along any section of the canal during the summer and the sheer number and variety of butterflies and dragonflies is impressive. Reports suggest that there are twenty-four species of butterfly and twenty species of dragonfly to be seen here. I was pleased to see both the comma, a variety of fritillary as well as the commoner, but nevertheless splendid, red admiral on most days of walking in September.

If you are interested in the wildlife along the K&A canal, the area is covered by three different wildlife trusts: the Avon Wildlife Trust (Bristol), the Wiltshire Trust for Nature Conservation (Devizes) and the Berkshire, Buckinghamshire & Oxfordshire Naturalist Trust (Oxford). The addresses of these organisations are given at the relevant place in the text. All, of course, welcome members as well as enquiries.

Walkers' Responsibilities

It seems amazing to me that anyone who buys a guide to the country needs to be told that they have to safeguard the thing they are planning to visit. But the piles of drink cans, broken down walls, fires during periods of drought and livestock wandering from an open gate all tell a different story. There's a lot of ill-feeling from walkers towards farmers who block rights of way or leave paths unmarked but perhaps we should try to limit the ill-feeling coming the other way by following a few simple rules.

1. Take all your rubbish home with you.
2. Keep to public footpaths and other rights of way when crossing privately owned land.
3. Fasten all gates.
4. Guard against all risk of fire.
5. Keep dogs under control especially near livestock.
6. Do not tamper with locks, swing bridges, canal or farm machinery, buildings or implements.
7. Avoid damage to walls, fences or crops.
8. Take care not to harm wildlife by trampling aimlessly across vegetation or into breeding sites, and don't dig up plants.

9. Park in proper car parks or with care so as not to block gates or prevent access.
10. If approached by a farmer or landowner, for whatever reason, be polite and smile.
11. Moored boats are private property and should be treated with respect.

❋ ❋ ❋

1: THE THAMES WALK
WESTMINSTER to READING

A full Thames Walk from central London to the source just beyond Cricklade has been the dream of ramblers for many years. Only now is the Countryside Commission putting the dream into reality and producing a full, coordinated and accessible path. The London-Bristol route takes advantage of the emerging Thames Walk for seventy-one and a half miles from Westminster to the outskirts of Reading. Apart from a tricky bit through some back streets of Wandsworth just after the beginning, the walk is good natured and easy. Most of the way it is impossible to believe that such massive urban sprawl is so close at hand. Although never wild, and never really very challenging, the route is full of interest and nearly always enjoyable.

A. WESTMINSTER to RICHMOND
Hammersmith is an approximate mid-way point.

Distance:	14 miles / 22 kilometres
Map:	OS Landranger 176 (West London)
Transport:	Westminster is on the Circle & District line of the London Underground. Hammersmith is on the District, Victoria and Metropolitan lines, and Richmond is on the District line (for return to Westminster). Richmond also has a BR main line station for trains to Waterloo or to destinations to the south-west (eg. Reading).
	The Green Line bus 718 joins London Victoria with Battersea Bridge, Putney, Kingston, Hampton Court, Walton, Weybridge, Staines and Windsor (all of which are on the Thames Walk). It runs hourly and is a limited stop.
Car Parks:	The best way of using the car is to park it in Richmond, take the tube to Westminster and then walk back.
	Westminster: Parking in central London is expensive, mostly by meter or privately owned car park, and is not recommended.

Hammersmith: NCP near church
Kew: Off Kew Green near gardens
Richmond: In centre and deer park

Tourist Info: Richmond on 081-892-0032

Sensible people will arrive at Westminster, take a snapshot of Big Ben's tower, disappear back down the tube station and get the first train to Putney Bridge in order to start the walk from there. The tedious trudge through Wandsworth's back streets aren't a great start to any long-distance walk but there again who said long-distance walkers are sensible?

The route starts at the Houses of Commons. If coming from the tube station, cross the road and then Westminster Bridge. On the other side, pass down some steps (right) to the Albert Embankment. After Lambeth Bridge, the route follows the road left of an office block. Turn right to cross the river at Vauxhall Bridge, then cross the road to continue along the right-hand (northern) bank of the river.

The walk now passes Battersea Power Station, Chelsea Bridge and the Royal Hospital before going under Albert Bridge (the fancy one). At Battersea Bridge, the path again changes banks. After crossing the river, follow the riverside walk signs right. A wall (belonging to a Rank Hovis factory) shortly pushes you left. Turn right along a road. After a church go right along Vicarage Walk (a riverside walk signpost shows the way) to pass some flats and the newish Chandler public house.

At the rail bridge bear left to a road, turn right and go under the railway. After about 300 yards, turn right at the traffic lights into York Road and walk for a further half a mile, passing a DIY store and Plantation Wharf (the brewery described in the RA book is being demolished). At a big road junction, bear right and then turn left down the pedestrian subway under the road. In the middle, bear right up to the other side (take the right-hand steps up). Turn left at the top of the steps to go along an unattractive narrow passage next to a Mercedes garage and a London Transport garage. Turn right at the end of this road. The route now gets even worse. This road passes a waste disposal site before going along a very unpromising track straight ahead. Amidst the corrugated iron and general dereliction, the path goes over the River Wandle and under a railway bridge. There has been some attempt to renovate the place here

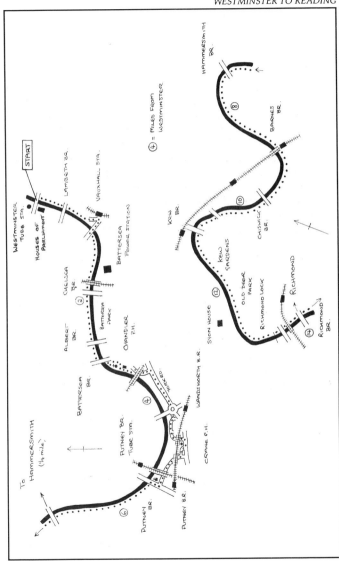

④ = MILES FROM WESTMINSTER

START

WESTMINSTER TUBE STA.

HOUSES OF PARLIAMENT

LAMBETH BR.

VAUXHALL STA.

BATTERSEA POWER STATION

CHELSEA BR.

ALBERT BR.

BATTERSEA PARK

③

CHANDLER P.H.

BATTERSEA BR.

PUTNEY BR. TUBE STA.

TO HAMMERSMITH (¼ MILE)

PUTNEY BR.

PUTNEY B.R.

⑥

④

WANDSWORTH B.R.

CRANE P.H.

SYON HOUSE

⑫

KEW GARDENS

OLD DEER PARK

RICHMOND LOCK

RICHMOND

RICHMOND BR.

⑭

KEW BR.

CHISWICK BR.

⑩

BARNES BR.

HAMMERSMITH BR.

⑧

19

Battersea Reach

including the installation of a London Wildlife Trust Reserve. Bear right at the road to pass the Crane pub. Turn right into Frogmore and then right again along Putney Bridge Road. After two railway bridges and just over half a mile of walking (you have the opportunity to see the river at Wandsworth Park if you wish), you reach a T-junction at Putney High Street. Turn right to reach Putney Bridge and the river. Cross the road opposite the church to finally rejoin the Thames towpath.

The walk from here is much improved, simpler to follow and generally more enjoyable (how could it not be?). At times there's almost a rural air about the place as we stroll alongside the route of the Oxford-Cambridge boat race.

The towpath is on the southern (left-hand) bank of the Thames. Start off along a road to reach a promenade and then a track. The way passes the Barn Elms reservoirs and the Harrod's depository before reaching Hammersmith Bridge.

Turn right here to reach the centre of Hammersmith (quarter of a mile) which is well stocked with shops and eating/drinking places, as well as tubes and buses to central London. Hammersmith is also the stopping place for a number of buses going west along the M3 and M4.

The path continues alongside Chiswick Reach to Barnes Bridge.

There are two pubs here. After passing under Chiswick Bridge (the boat race finish), the path reaches Kew Bridge. Turn left here for Kew Green (three pubs to choose from and several cafes and/or restaurants in the vicinity).

The walk is now very pleasant as it passes alongside Kew Gardens. To the right is Kew Palace and on the northern bank the entrance to the Grand Junction (Union) Canal. After Kew, the path passes Syon Park (on the right), the Old Deer Park, Richmond (on the left), and Isleworth Ait (island) on the right.

You will know that Richmond is getting close when you reach Richmond Lock (operated by the Port of London Authority). Pass under a road and then a railway bridge. At the next bridge, Richmond Bridge, turn left and left again. This road leads round right and then bears left to Richmond station. Both BR and London Underground are found in the same building.

Richmond is well-stocked with pubs, cafes and shops, and is easily reached by means of public transport - most notably the tube and the BR line.

B. RICHMOND to WEYBRIDGE
Hampton Court is an approximate mid-way point.

Distance:	14 miles/22 kilometres
Map:	OS Landranger 176 (West London)
Transport:	Richmond is on the District line of the Underground (for London) and has a BR main line for trains to Waterloo or to destinations to the south-west (eg. Reading).
	Weybridge is on mainline BR to Waterloo. To return to Richmond, you will need to change at Clapham Junction.
	Bus: LT 267 runs from Hampton Court to Kew and Hammersmith. The Green Line bus 718 may be useful (see part A above). The London & Country buses 427 & 437 go from Kingston via Weybridge to Staines. The 461 does a similar route to include Walton and Hampton Court terminating at Chertsey.
Car Parks:	Richmond: In centre and deer park Hampton Court: In Bushy Park Walton: Next to river at Walton Bridge Weybridge: In town centre and on-road in Thames Street

A thoroughly enjoyable and straightforward, if busy, section of the walk. Weekend strolling up and down the river is a popular pastime in these relatively affluent parts of south-west London - so expect crowds on nice days. Hampton Court is well worth a visit, if only to say that you got out of the maze in one piece.

The towpath maintains the southern (left-hand) bank all the way to Kingston Bridge. On the right is Marble Hill Park with its lovely white villa. The left-hand view quickly responds with Ham House, a National Trust property. After another one and a half miles, we reach Teddington Lock. From here on the Thames is no longer tidal. A further one and a half miles and the path reaches Kingston Bridge. Turn left here for the centre of the town and a railway station.

Kingston has numerous pubs and other places to eat and drink, as well as having the biggest shopping centre in the area.

At Kingston, the walk switches to the northern bank by means of Kingston Bridge. Turn left down to the Barge Walk which now runs around the perimeter of Hampton Court Park. After about two miles, the path reaches the entrance to Hampton Court and Hampton Court Bridge.

There is a pub on the bridge and a cafe in the grounds of Hampton Court itself (entrance to the grounds is free). Turn left over the bridge for Hampton Court BR station, a small number of shops and for bus stops.

After lunch, cross the bridge and carry on along the path which has now returned to the southern bank. Our way passes through Hurst Park and by the Molesey reservoirs before reaching Sunbury Lock. After the Anglers Inn and Walton Bridge, the walker has the choice of either taking the direct route along a new (well, 1930s) straight navigational cut, the Desborough Cut, or pursuing the purist route around some meanders in the river (crossing by means of bridges at both ends). Both return to the same spot just outside Weybridge and Shepperton Lock.

After Desborough Cut, the path reaches D'Oyly Carte Island (with its high footbridge). Shortly thereafter, a ferry leaves from this side of the river to connect with the towpath which continues on the opposite bank. If you wish to continue the walk to Chertsey (by simply turning left and following the river), ring the bell provided (following the instructions). It's worth noting that I've rung the bell

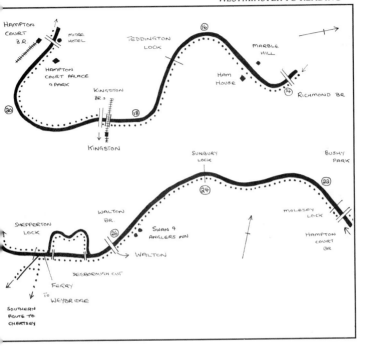

here several times without response. If this happens, you will have to take the southerly route which leaves the river and doesn't return until Chertsey.

If taking the southern route or stopping in Weybridge, carry on along the path to reach Thames Street. For stoppers, this road goes directly into the centre of Weybridge. Most buses stop outside the Ship Hotel which you will meet on the right just before the shops. The BR station is just over a mile south of the river. Carry on through the main shopping street and bear left at a roundabout near St. James' Church. Keep straight on at two further junctions to walk up a hill along a main road through woodland. The station will (eventually) be found on the right.

Those wishing to continue along the southern path should walk as far as the Old Crown pub. Take the alley to the side (next to the

23

public WC), continue across a road and then after 100 yards turn right in front of some cottages to a green and white footbridge. At the next small road, turn half left to go along another alley to reach the Wey Navigation at a lock (canal fans note!). Cross the bridge, turn left and walk for about half a mile until you meet a brick bridge. Take the first opportunity to cross a small brook to the right to a minor road. Turn right up this road (ie back the way you've come) to a fork in the road. Follow the footpath sign left, over a stile to a field. Cross the field to a caravan site. Turn right and cross a stile to a footpath sign. Turn left for about two yards and then right to walk with a ditch on the right. Reach a gap in the hedge and follow the clear path across the field to another sign which points left to a bridge. Cross the bridge and turn left to walk along the side of the field. After quarter of a mile or so, a signpost points right across the field to a minor road. This is Chertsey Meads. Turn half left (not on the metalled road) and take a clear path across the meadow to an alley with a marina on the left. (There is access, joy oh joys, to the river just before the alley). The route then gives the impression of trespassing but doesn't as it takes a course between factories and out to a road next to Chertsey Bridge.

C. WEYBRIDGE to WINDSOR

Runnymede is an approximate mid-way point.

Distance:	14 miles / 22 kilometres
Map:	OS Landranger 176 (West London)
Transport:	Weybridge is on mainline BR to Waterloo. Windsor has two stations, one in the middle of town and the other near the river at Windsor Bridge (on the way to Eton). Trains from Riverside station go to Staines for connections to Weybridge.
	Buses: The Green Line bus 718 will be useful as it connects Windsor, Staines and Weybridge at hourly intervals. The London & Country buses 427 & 437 go from Weybridge to Staines. The 411 goes from Staines to Windsor.
Car Parks:	Weybridge: Signposted in town
	Chertsey Meads: Several places around the open meadows
	Runnymede: Near Magna Carta Island
	Windsor: Large well-signposted parks in town
Tourist Info:	Windsor: 0753-852010 (at the central BR station)

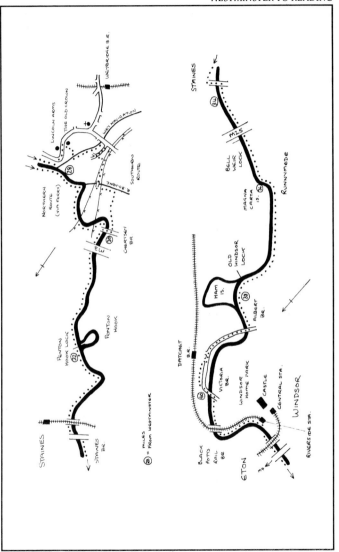

The route out of Weybridge is tedious and nowhere near the river. However, if you can avoid tripping over American tourists, Runnymede is pleasant and the final section into Windsor is good.

If you've arrived by bus or car, I suggest that you walk down Thames Street until you reach the Old Crown and turn left to take the alley route described at the end of the last section. From the BR station you might take a slightly quicker route. Turn left outside the station and go down the hill until you reach a roundabout near a church. Turn left here. Walk on to cross the Wey Navigation (this is the brick bridge mentioned in the previous route). The minor metalled road right is the road which those coming from the river have to cross a ditch for, so walk up here until the road forks right and take the signpost footpath left to continue as already described.

At Chertsey Bridge, cross to the northern bank to pass Chertsey Lock and go under the M3. The route then stays close to the river and by-passes Laleham to Penton Hook Lock. There now follows about two to two and a half miles of pleasant buildings to Staines Railway Bridge. Bear right briefly along the road and into town, then turn back down left to the river bank at Staines Bridge. The town centre has plenty of pubs, shops, buses and BR station (Reading-Waterloo line).

Cross the river at the road bridge and turn right. The path now goes under the M25 and alongside Bell Weir Lock. After bending sharply left and then right, we reach Runnymede. There is a cafe here. The path briefly goes onto pavement but then returns to the river bank to pass through Old Windsor.

Keep close to the riverside and avoid paths going off left. The towpath follows a new cut left (the main river goes around a loop surrounding Windsor sewage works). This rejoins the river at a weir. Cross the river at the next road bridge - Albert Bridge. Windsor Great Park occupies the view on the left. There is now a boring stretch along the road into Datchet. At the end of the village, a signpost takes us off the road but parallel to it for a short distance. Return to the road after quarter of a mile to cross the river again at Victoria Bridge.

There is now a fine view of Windsor Castle. After crossing the bridge, turn down right to rejoin the towpath. This follows the river round under Black Potts railway bridge and on to Romney Lock.

Continue past the boatyard and go down a lane left to a red brick tower. Bear right down Romney Walk. This ends at Windsor Bridge. Turn left and follow the road round to the castle, central station and the main shopping areas.

Windsor is very touristy but seems to manage. As a consequence, it has plenty of places to eat and drink, as well as a range of accommodation. Buses leave from stops opposite the castle. If you wish to return to Weybridge or Staines by train, you should use the Riverside Station. Central Station (opposite the castle) only has trains to Slough (and hence to London or Reading).

D. WINDSOR to MARLOW

Maidenhead is an approximate mid-way point.

Distance:	13¹/₂ miles/21 kilometres
Map:	OS Landranger 175 (Reading & Windsor)
Transport:	A difficult stretch. Windsor is on the BR branch line from Slough. Marlow is also on a branch line, this time from Maidenhead. Connections are therefore possible but time-consuming on weekdays; impossible on Sundays. Buses: There are no buses between Windsor & Marlow and no easy connections. There are, however, regular services to High Wycombe, Henley and Reading.
Car Parks:	Windsor/Maidenhead: Well signposted in-town parks Maidenhead: Near river on Cookham road near Boulter's Lock Cookham: Small car park on outskirts of town Marlow: Town centre and near BR station
Tourist Info:	Marlow: 06284-3597 Maidenhead: 0628-781110

A section noteworthy for the route's steepest climb at Winter Hill (assuming you don't intend to walk up to the Clifton Suspension Bridge at the Bristol end). A pleasant stroll and on sunny, winter weekends, the Cookham section is a positive stream of walking boots and bobble hats.

From Windsor Central BR station, walk out to the castle. Turn left and follow this road as it bends first right and then left to reach Windsor Bridge. If coming from Riverside station, turn right and

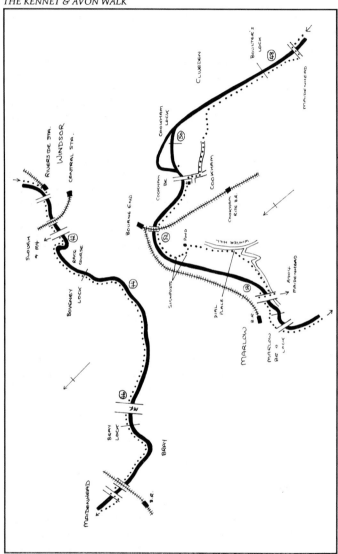

right again. Straight ahead is Eton. Cross the (pedestrianised) bridge and pass down left to continue the walk on the northern bank of the river.

Within a short distance the path passes under a railway bridge and then the main A332 which carries Windsor's traffic to the M4. After passing Boveney Lock and following the river for approximately four miles, the route goes under the M4 and passes Bray (not a vicar in sight). The river now bends left and then right to arrive at Maidenhead. The first indication of this is Brunel's famous railway bridge.

At Maidenhead Road Bridge the path crosses to the other bank.

At the bridge, there are pubs on both sides of the river. Turn left at the bridge for the town centre (farther than you think), which has the usual range of shops and enough roundabouts to keep most people busy for a while.

After Maidenhead Bridge follow the road for a couple of hundred yards. At the Thames Hotel it is safe to cross to a river path. Pass a tea kiosk and a car park before reaching Boulter's Lock at Boulter's Inn. A bit farther on, when the road goes left, bear right through a gate. On the far bank are the grounds of the National Trust property, Cliveden.

This is a beautiful stretch of quiet, leafy riverside. Wonderful. Just on the point where the woodland clears on the left, Cliveden house and clock tower can be seen straight ahead on the hill.

Before Cookham, the path is forced left near a derelict landing stage (just opposite two cottages on the far bank). This path winds through woodland until you reach a stile. At that point make for the house half left and an alley which eventually leads round to a metalled road (Mill Lane) near the entrance to some houses. Turn left and then right along a more major road and into Cookham.

Cookham has a number of eating and drinking places but is short of stocking-up places. The Stanley Spencer Museum will be passed on the left.

Continue on this road (do not turn left for anything but shopping or lunching) until you see a sign left for the church (if you reach the bridge you've gone too far). Go through the churchyard and back to the river. Turn left. The path now makes a gradual bend right and passes under Bourne End Rail Bridge. The towpath changes sides just after the river has turned back left, so we have to go in for some deviation. At a white house, a signpost points half left to another post which points even farther left across a field. This route leads shortly to the bottom of Winter Hill. After passing a pond, cross a stile and turn right to climb the hill using a very clear unmade road. This eventually reaches a metalled road. Turn right. Ignore turnings off until you reach an area of car parking at the top of the hill.

Continue along the road until you reach Dial Place, where you should take a gravel drive to the right of the entrance. Similarly go right of the entrance to Rivendell house down a very narrow track. Bear right in the woods to meet a road. Turn immediately right here and down steps to join another road. This bears right to go over a stream towards a dual carriageway (A404) with its huge bridge over the Thames.

When nearly at the bridge, take the steps that go up to the road. Turn right to cross the river. On the other side go down some steps on the right to reach the river bank again. Turn right under the road bridge. Walk along the river until you reach a field and then some housing when the path is forced to turn right to join a road. Turn left. This road bends right to go close to the river and a fine view to Marlow Bridge. After a right turn, go left into a narrow (brick-wall-lined) alley which eventually leads to a road. Cross the road and go down another alley opposite the Two Brewers pub. This leads to a church and a road. Turn left here for Marlow Bridge and the river, and right for the town centre.

Marlow has a small but adequate shopping centre. For the BR station, turn right at the church and then first right after a confectionery shop. This road runs for quarter of a mile, passing two pubs before you turn half right to go along Station Approach. Trains run hourly except Sundays, when they don't run at all. Buses to Henley and Reading or to High Wycombe stop at the very end of this main shopping street.

E. MARLOW to READING

Henley is an approximate mid-way point.

Distance:	16½ miles/26 kilometres
Map:	OS Landranger 175 (Reading & Windsor)
Transport:	Both Marlow and Reading have mainline BR stations that

connect via Maidenhead. The bus is far easier. Beeline 327, 328 & 329 run from Reading to Marlow (via Henley) at half-hourly intervals weekdays, two hourly on Sundays. Enquiries to: 0734-581358

Car Parks: Marlow, Henley & Reading have signposted in-town car parks
Hurley: Largish area near church
Lower Shiplake & Sonning: On-road

Tourist Info: Reading: 0734-566719

An excellent walk from Marlow to just after Sonning (ie. until you hit Reading). By that stage you're only about two miles from Reading centre (one and a half from the entrance to the K&A canal), so grit the teeth and carry on to the end. But save the rest for a warm summer's day.

From Marlow Bridge turn right along the northern bank. Cross the river at a new footbridge just after Temple Lock, turn right and carry on to Hurley. Cross the footbridge to the lock island and back again via another bridge at the other end. The village of Hurley is very pleasant and offers a pub, the Rabbit, and a shop.

The path now goes through some popular barbeque spots and next to a caravan park before reaching a meandering section. On the opposite bank are the laboratories of the Water Research Centre. Here the towpath changes sides again. However, we can continue alongside the river for about another half mile.

After a small footbridge (with stiles), a footpath sign points away from the river to the corner of the field. Go right of the gate and over the stile to a farm track. Turn right and follow the track to some buildings. Just after the track divides, take the stile between the two new paths. Walk beside the fence. To the left is Culham Court. Maintain the same straight course to pass to the left of some more buildings and out to a road. Turn right to pass the Flowerpot public house. This road (Ferry Lane) goes down to the river, where the path continues left. After half a mile, the path reaches Hambleden Mill with its impressive weir.

You can cross here but there are no shops or watering holes within easy reach on the other side. There is, however, a car park on the Hambleden village road (quarter of a mile).

The river now makes a very gentle left turn, passing Temple

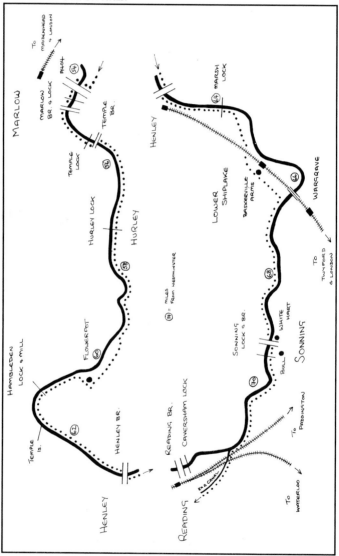

Houses of Parliament

Desborough Cut

Blake's Lock Museum

Southcote Lock

Island (with its white folly) and on to Henley (about two miles after the mill).

Henley has a pleasant centre with a number of shops, a goodly number of pubs and several cafes. The railway station is well signposted. Buses run to Marlow and Reading.

Cross Henley Bridge and turn left to walk along the pavement to a point where the road turns right. The path carries straight on alongside a park. After about a mile, our way goes across a wooden causeway alongside a weir and Marsh Lock. From there it returns to the northern bank and out to a field. After a short distance we have to divert inland. Bear right at the end of the field to pass down a fenced path and out to a road. Follow this round, bearing left at a junction and along a pleasant road with big houses on both sides. Some way down there will be a hedged path off right. This crosses the BR line and goes into a minor road which then leads to a junction (shop and pub here, for BR station turn left). This is Lower Shiplake.

Carry straight on along Mill Road. When this comes to a T-junction, turn left and then right along a path to the river and Shiplake Lock. The towpath has now returned to this side of the river, so turn right to continue the walk.

The way to Sonning, about two and a half miles farther on, is simple and trouble free. After passing over a footbridge, turn left to cross Sonning Bridge and turn right to go along the southern bank.

Sonning has a small shop, a cafe, two pubs and an up-market restaurant. The first pub is here at the bridge; the second, the Bull, can be found near the churchyard.

The way now passes Sonning Lock. The view to the right includes extensive flooded gravel diggings and, within a mile, the outskirts of Reading to the left. About two miles from Sonning, Reading gas works will be clearly in view left. Shortly thereafter the Kennet & Avon Canal leaves the Thames to pass under a Brunel railway bridge.

This is the start of the K&A Walk to Bristol. Those wishing to continue immediately should turn left in person and to the first part of the K&A Walk in this book. To reach the centre of Reading, it is easiest to follow the K&A as far as High Bridge before turning right into town. If you wish to avoid the K&A for now, or want to get to the bus or railway station, cross the rickety U-shaped footbridge that goes over the canal and continue along the Thames path. Soon you will meet a road bridge (Reading Bridge). Go up to the road and turn left. Continue straight ahead under the railway and turn right at the next roundabout. Pass in front of a new, pinkish, tower block. The railway station is now on the right. The bus station can be found on the left a little farther on.

Reading has plenty of shops, cafes and pubs but little cheap accommodation.

2: THE K & A WALK
READING to WOOLHAMPTON

Although the thought of walking through Reading doesn't sound particularly appealing, the canal and the various sights around it make it surprisingly pleasant and interesting. Town-haters will, of course, find it hard going but will soon be relieved as the route quickly reaches the low-lying water meadows around Burghfield and then on to the old Bath Road coach-stop village of Theale. The route then continues through the outskirts of Sulhamsted and Aldermaston to Woolhampton.

This is the oldest section of the Kennet and Avon Canal. The portion from Reading to Newbury was formerly called the Kennet Navigation and was opened in 1723. It was eventually bought (for a cool £100,000) by the K&A Canal Company following the completion of the Newbury to Bath section in 1810.

The route runs close to the A4 and the BR Reading-Newbury line throughout. This allows a positive plethora of starting or stopping points. Buses are frequent and even run on Sundays. Trains are less common and don't stop at Woolhampton's Midgham station on Sundays.

Reading is a major shopping centre and walkers should take advantage of it while they can. Theale has a small number of shops including a small supermarket. Woolhampton, meanwhile, only has a small village shop. The route is well provided with pubs all the way along.

A. READING to THEALE

Distance:	7 miles/11 kilometres
Map:	OS Landranger 175 (Reading & Windsor)
Transport:	BR Reading & Theale (0734-595911)
	Bee Line Buses (0734-581358) nos. 102 & 103 run half-hourly along A4 (Sundays every two to three hours)
Car Parks:	Reading: Multi-storey in central Reading
	Limited on-road in Newtown (Cemetery Junction) area
	Burghfield: Roadside near Burghfield Bridge
	Theale: On-road in town centre and near swing bridge
	Station car park
Tourist Info:	Reading on 0734-566719

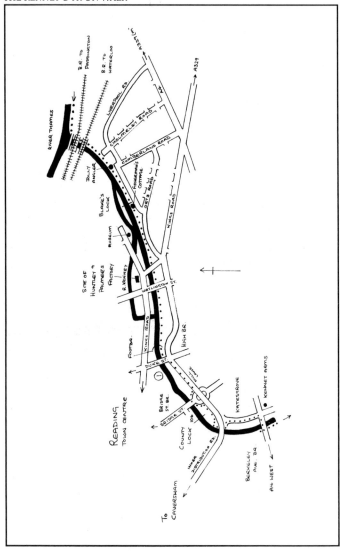

The canal begins where the River Kennet flows into the Thames at Newtown. The OS map reference is 731739. This is to the east of central Reading and not far from the Reading end of the A329M motorway which links this side of the town with the M4.

Car drivers can either try to park close to the Thames in the Newtown/Cemetery Junction area or they can use one of the many, and well signposted, town centre multi-storey car parks.

The simple, non-repetitive route from town for either car drivers or those arriving by public transport starts at the railway station. Leave the station and turn immediately left. The route passes in front of a pink-coloured tower block, the Apex Plaza. At the large roundabout turn left towards Caversham and go under the railway bridge. Cross the road and turn right at the next roundabout before Reading Bridge House. About 200 yards on the left are the King's Meadow playing fields. Bear left across the fields until you reach the Thames. You are now on the Thames towpath. Turn right (downstream) and walk for about three quarters of a mile until you reach a river coming in from the right (the south) under a railway bridge. This is the River Kennet and the start of the K&A Canal Walk.

It's an inauspicious start. Wedged between the gas works and some graffiti-covered, derelict buildings, the Kennet does its best to look welcoming - not easy under the circumstances. The sheets of rusty metal, the empty lemonade bottles and some blood-stained bandage don't help photographers but I took a snap anyway. Don't get too disheartened - it does improve. As if to encourage me (at least), the augurs threw up a canal boat turning into the Kennet, an Inter-City 125 going over the railway bridge and Concorde deafening everything from above. Three ages of transport? The advancement of communications? The unstoppable march of dehumanising progress? It must have meant something. I decided not to think about it and started on my way.

Walkers from the station should now cross the Kennet by means of the footbridge (thoughfully added in 1891) to make their first steps along the K&A on the southern bank. Go under the railway bridge.

The first railway bridge here is a listed building! It was opened in 1840 and forms part of Brunel's Great Western Railway route from Paddington to Bristol. It seems ironic that the very first thing you meet on the K&A

Walk carries the means for the death of the canal as a commercial enterprise. After the opening of the full GWR line in June 1841, the decline of the canal as a going concern was both dramatic and inevitable.

The route passes under a huge gas pipe and a second railway bridge (the Reading to Guildford/Waterloo line). For those in need of provisions, Cumberland Road (the second road to the left) has a corner shop about 200 yards on the right. Back on the K&A those of a thirsty disposition can drop into the Jolly Angler public house situated so close to the canal that late evening drinking must present quite a risk. Almost opposite the Kennet proper leaves the canal and makes its own way to a weir. We, meanwhile, continue on a fairly straight course, passing some new houses on our left and a lock to the right.

It should be admitted at this point that we haven't reached the K&A Canal proper yet and that this section is still under the jurisdiction of the National Rivers Authority. Blake's Lock is operated by them and not by the people who normally run the canals, namely the British Waterways Board. We reach BWB territory in about a mile's 'time'.

For those who continue to have a thirst, you will pass the Fisherman's Cottage public house just a few yards from the lock on the left.

With first the Jolly Angler and then the Fisherman's Cottage, readers will think that this is a popular spot for fishing. Walkers will already have come to that conclusion as they step over the endless piles of tackle strewn across the path. Interspersed with moth-eaten buddleia bushes, the fishermen stared patiently down at the water, hoping, praying perhaps, for some sort of movement on their lines. I didn't actually see anyone catch anything although, unsolicited, an old man came up to me and said that he used to fish here seventy years ago. Desirous of something original for this page, I asked him whether the place had changed much. Instead of answering he simply wandered off towards the Thames. I, in turn, decided that there must be more to this oral history business than meets the eye and went in the opposite direction.

We now pass some new housing to the left. Here the River Kennet returns briefly to meet the canal on the opposite bank. Across the broadening expanse of water is Blake's Lock Museum and Reading Marine.

The museum, which contains some bits of Reading's history, together, when I went, with an exhibition of old photographs of the K&A Canal, is open from 10am-5pm weekdays and 2pm-5pm weekends. Entry is free. If getting there without a boat looks impossible, I can now reveal that if you go along to the next bridge (Kings Road Bridge), up on to the road, turn right and then right again (along Gasworks Road), you will find the museum on your right.

The towpath continues under Kings Road Bridge to the third watering hole in under a mile - the Wharf Wine Press. If you do this section at opening time, this first mile could take all day! Take advantage of the seats just here on the left to read the next piece of information.

Raise the name of Reading in polite company and they will probably be able to tell you three things about the place: it has a railway station (most trains going west stop here), it has a gaol (Oscar Wilde 'visited' here in 1896-7, although he didn't write his 'Ballad of...' until some time later) and it makes biscuits. If you're sitting on one of the recommended seats, Huntley & Palmer biscuit factory is now staring you in the face. In Victorian times, this was THE number one biscuit company in the country. By the turn of the century they were the biggest employer in Reading and sold their wares around the world. It was Huntley & Palmer who started the idea of selling an 'assortment' in specially made and decorated tins. The company had a liking for the canal - seemingly water transport resulted in fewer broken biscuits! George Palmer himself was a great benefactor to the town and many areas and buildings in Reading still bear his name. Now, sadly, Huntley & Palmer is only one part of a huge conglomerate (Nabisco) and they stopped making biscuits here in 1977. The building (put up in 1937) used to be just the front of a huge factory but is now reduced to offices and will shortly be further reduced to rubble. Now, doesn't that take the biscuit.

The path passes under Watlington Street Bridge. Here 'flats' have started to be called 'luxury apartments' and a lot of recent development has been undertaken. We quickly pass over a self-styled 'narrow bridge'. On the far bank the Kennet rejoins us after its sojourn into the old part of Reading and the remains of Reading Abbey.

If the artist's impression is correct, the abbey must have been a grand place with twin towers fronting a huge cathedral-like building. Henry I endowed it (after his only legitimate son drowned off the French coast in

1120) and Thomas à Becket consecrated it in 1168. The abbot and the monks were given numerous rights and possessions and the abbey dominated the area for 400 years. Henry was buried here - although precisely where isn't clear. John of Gaunt (son of Edward III) was married here. Others stayed or held events here. Henry VIII, of course, wasn't a great fan of monasteries, and in 1539 the abbot was executed and systematic demolition of the building begun. Only some tatty-looking walls and an inner gateway are left. The latter is notable because it once housed the Abbey School for Girls and, in the late eighteenth century, one of those girls was Jane Austen.

The path continues through an area of recent development. On the left is an almost reasonable-looking multi-storey car park. Pedestrians can cross the canal here using an iron footbridge. We carry on to the stone High (or Dukes) Bridge, which carries Duke Street across the canal. By the way, it may seem like more - particularly if you've been in all three bars - but you have now completed one whole mile of the K&A Walk!

Those who wish to stock up on provisions, have a cup of tea or visit the public conveniences should now turn right and walk into central Reading (200 yards). The town centre is chock-a-block with all manner of places to eat as well as shops of all descriptions. There will not be another opportunity to do any of these things until the Cunning Man pub at Burghfield Bridge (three and a half miles) or Theale (six miles).

This is one of Reading's oldest areas and traditionally the centre of the town's business and administration. To the east of the bridge was the town wharf (High Bridge Wharf) active in times long before the Kennet Navigation. In the sixteenth century, the wharf was used for unloading goods which were then carried up to the market place 200 yards to the north. A council document records trading in fish (and shellfish) and cheese, as well as 'roots, onions and such like'. The present High Bridge replaced an old timber bridge in 1787. It was called High Bridge because it was taller than the old one. Clever eh? The importance of this shouldn't be underestimated though because until then the bigger barges had to stop here to unload. The new bridge meant they could go farther for the first time. The bridge cost the council £3,500 and its building formed part of a general spruce-up that the town went though at the end of the eighteenth century. Apparently it needed it desperately.

On the other side of the bridge, where there is now a thoroughly ugly car park, stood Yield Hall. In Henry VIII's time, this housed the merchant guild. It's said that the noise made by women doing their washing on the banks of the Kennet disturbed the merchants' meetings. One wonders what they would have felt about the din from the cars, buses and lorries that now pass along Duke Street.

At Duke Street the route turns left as there is no public access along the canal between High Bridge and the next bridge along - Bridge Street Bridge. Walkers should cross Duke Street, and turn left to meet a dual carriageway road. This is Mill Street. Turn right and walk in front of the bus station. The dual carriageway flyover should be on your left. After about 200 yards, Bridge Street can be found on the right.

Mill Street seems grossly misnamed; the impression of a quietly flowing mill stream conflicts horribly with the fumes and noise of the inner distribution road. Nevertheless an old mill once stood here on the site of the bus station. In fact there were once a large number of mills along the Kennet, all taking advantage of the plentiful supply of fast running water. In the Middle Ages the town was an established centre for cloth manufacture. Fulling mills processed the woven cloth by beating it underwater to make it shrink (to give it strength and thickness) and then cleaning it with a type of clay called, appropriately, fuller's earth.

In Elizabethan times there were seven bridges on Bridge Street between here and St Mary's Church (about quarter of a mile up the road). As the Kennet was tamed and channelled so the number of bridges needed declined. By 1611 it only had five. It now has only one, and if you stand on it and look back towards High Bridge, the bus station will be on your right. On the left, William Simonds's brewery was built in 1790. It was the Simonds company that bought the towpath between here and Duke Street (in the 1880s) and closed it. It narrowed the channel, making it deeper and more treacherous for barges. It was also renamed; this section is called 'Brewery Gut'. The name isn't a pertinent description of the effects of the brewing trade - a 'gut' is actually a narrow water-passage or strait. Alas, like Huntley & Palmer before it, William Simonds became part of a large conglomerate in 1960 (this time it was Courage). This area is presently derelict, Courage having moved its brewing facilities to a site close to the M4 in 1977. The buildings to the west of Bridge Street are, however, quite historic and still standing - if only just.

Bridge Street Bridge itself was once a severe obstacle to traffic passing along the canal. In 1946 girders were put in to strengthen the bridge with

*the result that the headroom was reduced from 8'6" to 4'6". If a barge
wanted to go underneath, the water level had to be lowered and the boat had
to take on iron ballast. When the bridge was inspected in 1963, it was shown
that the girders weren't supporting the bridge at all and they were taken
away in 1966.*

*The canal at this point (and onwards), by the way, is under the
jurisdiction of the British Waterways Board and hence is officially classified
as a canal. Does it look any different to you? Honestly?*

Our way will shortly be blocked again but firstly we'll take a
quick detour down to County Lock. Ignore the main pedestrian
route which runs off left alongside the flyover and take the dirt path
that runs between a ditch and a car park. This is a dead end but quite
a pleasant spot to sit and watch boats navigate their way through a
typical lock.

*County Lock is the first (or last) lock on the K&A. Each lock is
numbered in sequence from the Bristol end. County Lock is No. 106.*

*Locks have been used on rivers since the Middle Ages as gateways
through weirs. The original type was called a flash lock, not because it
looked good, but because it was simply an obstruction which could be lifted
out of the way allowing a flash of water to pass through, hopefully with the
boat on it. Locks with mitred gates are reputed to have been designed by
Leonardo da Vinci, and the first British lock of this design dates from 1566
(on the River Exe). This type of lock, called the pound lock, could be
negotiated without the dramatic loss of water that was characteristic of the
flash lock. The length of water between the locks, by the way, is called a
pound. The operation of a lock is remarkably simple but still makes an
irresistible spectator sport.*

To continue the route, return to the roundabout and turn right
to walk up the pedestrian pathway. The flyover should be on your
left. After about seventy-five yards take the steps down right and
walk underneath the flyover. This is yet another popular spot for
fishermen. At the end of the bridge the pathway turns away from
the canal. The towpath is now on the other side.

Walk 'inland' alongside the broken TV sets, upturned
supermarket trolleys and old Coke tins and take the first opportunity
to turn right. This is Katesgrove Road. Pass a school on the left and
Phoebe Court on the right. Turn right at the traffic lights. As you
cross Berkeley Avenue Bridge, you will see a post with the towpath

waymark on it on the right. Go down the steps to the north bank of the canal.

Keenies will want to retrace their steps to the point where they left the canal (albeit on the other side). Those in a hurry to get out of town will turn immediately right and go for it!

It may not look like it now but Katesgrove was once a hive of industry. There were iron foundries, and brickworks as well as the cloth manufacturers mentioned previously. Sailcloth made in Katesgrove was used by the Royal Navy during the Napoleonic wars.

The path now winds its way along a tight-fitting track. On the southern bank the gardens of the terrace houses run down to the canal. On the right we pass some warehouses.,

To those who prefer their walks to be in the fresh air and peace of the countryside, this section must be a blessed relief. Okay, it's scrubby and a bit untidy but for those who started at Reading, this is their first sight of country. At the right time of year you'll see dragonflies and when I was there the purple loosestrife added a pleasant dash of colour. You'll also see, surprise, surprise, a few fishermen. Except this time there really was a surprise - I actually saw a fish being caught! Everybody, including me, seemed rather dumb struck at this highly unexpected event and not totally sure what to do next.

This part of Reading is bereft of houses and factories for a very good reason - the Kennet. The land is boggy and ill-draining and difficult to build on. It's to be regretted that modern technology is able to solve the problem. These low-lying water meadows are an excellent antidote to the sprawl that Reading has become.

The route continues under Rose Kiln Lane Bridge (site of another brickworks). The strange blue building in the distance belongs to Thames Water Authority. In high summer, the K&A disappears to our left, hidden behind a mass of vegetation. As Foudry Brook carries on south, the K&A turns west and we, of course, go with it. The route passes the Thames Water building and does a quick zig-zag around Fobney Lock Bridge and Fobney Lock itself. The path has now moved to the southern (left-hand) bank. Being brought up correctly, I won't mention the sewage filter beds on the northern side of the canal at this point.

There now follows a long straight stretch called Fobney Cut which ends in a bridge crossing a weir. The path now bears slightly

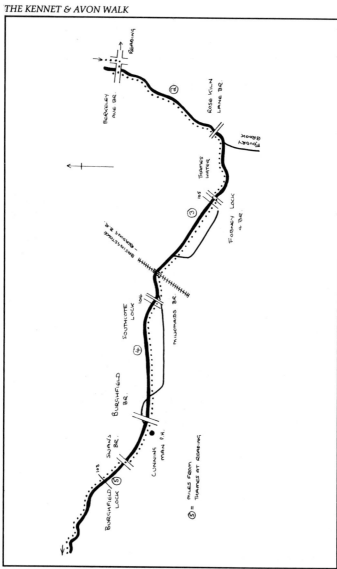

BERKELEY AVE BR.

READING

ROSE KILN LANE BR.

FOBNEY BROOK

(2) = MILES FROM THAMES AT READING

THAMES WATER

105

③

FOBNEY LOCK & BR.

BASINGSTOKE READING BR.

SOUTHCOTE LOCK

104

MILKMAIDS BR.

④

BURGHFIELD BR.

SWANS BR.

CUNNING MAN P.H.

BURGHFIELD LOCK

103

⑤

ⓢ = MILES FROM THAMES AT READING

right and passes under the Reading-Basingstoke railway.

Now's the time, you think, for some placid contemplation: the meaning of life, the state of the country, the state of the bank balance, but no... A large area of south Reading has been dug and removed in the name of gravel. Interestingly this has added a lot to the area. Not only do naturalists get excellent bird habitats but water sport enthusiasts get all the sailing and water-skiing areas their hearts desire. It's just that it's very noisy to dig up. Here just south of Southcote Lock, trucks and diggers were hard at it. And next to them a cacophony of cable hurtling electricity in, or it could be out, of Reading. It seems that we must continue just a little further for our solitude.

Take the small footbridge over the river Kennet and back onto the south bank of the canal. Ignore the prettily named Milkmaid's Foot Bridge which passes over the canal. Carry on to Southcote Lock (spelt Southcot on the lock itself).

The sign also tells you that this is lock No. 104; not great encouragement to those who have already had enough. The small Victorian building next to the lock is Southcote Pumping Station. It was opened in 1850 and once pumped water into Reading.

Continue along the overgrown path and across a weir. This one is labelled 'Drowning black spot - many people have died here.' A little further on a tributary goes off the canal to the north.

The resultant island is Burghfield Island and is a popular mooring spot. If you haven't seen any barges so far, you are almost certain to see some here as this is home of the Burghfield Island Boat Club. The owners are proud of their boats and say so in bright, strident colours. It's a real delight to see them and difficult to resist rummaging though the rucksack for the camera.

The path now goes under Burghfield Bridge. The Cunning Man pub is on the left and a small gate is conveniently placed for walkers. If you're thirsty now remember that there's still three miles to the centre of Theale.

As you sip your drink, you might consider the excitement that occurred here while the canal was being built. It would be true to say that the canal wasn't universally popular. Although the towns and villages from Newbury westwards were all in favour, the people of Reading were not. They felt that they would lose control of the transport and distribution of goods to the south-west of the county. Others felt that fiddling about with the Kennet would ruin the water for milling purposes. Shop- and innkeepers felt that they would lose custom from visitors who came to pick up their goods from the Thames wharves.

These concerns were not merely expressed verbally in the local pubs. When the canal builders got to Burghfield in 1720, the hostility of the townsfolk broke into violence with 300 angry people swarming across the fields and deliberately smashing up parts of the canal works. The canal company asked the Mayor and Recorder of Reading to take legal action - only to find that they had both been in the mob!

The mayor promised to keep the peace but the people thought differently. Threatening letters were sent to bargemasters and passing barges were pelted with stones. Further outbreaks of violence occurred in 1725 and workers making repairs during the following winter were arrested by Reading Corporation as rioters!

The whole business smouldered on for several years. By 1733 the company had got around to paying compensation for damage caused during the building of the canal. By 1740 the people of Reading seemed to have realised that the navigation brought prosperity rather than lost it and the whole issue disappeared into history.

After passing a fresh gravel pit on the southern side, the towpath swaps to the northern bank of the canal at Swan's Footbridge.

The pill box positioned at the northern end of Swan's Bridge is the first of many that will be seen along the K&A. During the Second World War the canal was seen as a useful anti-tank defence in the event of a German invasion. The pill boxes were built as guard posts. Venturing inside is not for the faint-hearted as the smell is a clear indication of their present use.

Burghfield Lock is found within a hundred yards of the footbridge.

Burghfield Lock, which looks in such good order now, epitomises the problems faced by those who run the canal and those who have so successfully sought to restore it. The lock was declared unsafe in June 1950 and closed. It was partially re-built and re-opened in March 1952. In 1955 the bottom sill cracked and it again became inoperable. Following further building work, the lock was re-opened in 1959. In early 1965 the bottom gates collapsed and the lock was again closed. With the sterling efforts of the K&A Canal Trust (and some help from the Royal Engineers) the lock was repaired and back in action before the end of the year. And this happens to nearly all the locks nearly all the time!

Just after the lock and through the trees on the left-hand (southern) side is Burghfield Mill. There was mention of a mill at Burghfield in the Domesday book. The present structure was once a flour mill and in the last days of its life was used to mill cocoa. It then declined to the ignominy of being just a store.

The path now passes through a narrow, overgrown track and out to an open field (Harrick Meadow). Here the canal bends and twists, and navigation maps warn bargemasters to take care. The value of this became evident when I passed a barge trying to disentangle itself from the bank. The lucky walker has a choice - to follow the bends or take the direct, straight route which leads, after a pill box on our right, to Hissey's Bridge. Once more the towpath changes sides. Once over the bridge, immediately turn right. Here the bank sports trees and we lose sight of the canal for a minute. However, our target is clear. It is the massive grey slabs that constitute the bridge carrying the M4 motorway.

The noise of the M4 will have been evident for the last ten minutes. I didn't mention it earlier for fear of depressing you. I suggest that you use this opportunity to be grateful that you're here on the K&A canal path and not up there commuting or doing battle with juggernauts and headlight-flashing company reps.

The towpath passes under the M4 and on through a relatively young plantation of trees. On the left Theale Lake (an old gravel pit) is used for water sports. The canal bends slightly northwards and we follow it to another pill box next to Garston Lock.

Mention Garston Lock to a lock connoisseur and see his eyes light up. Garston is an example of a turf-sided lock. As we'll meet another one just after Thatcham, I'll save the explanation until then. The thought of that will no doubt speed your passage.

As I stood admiring Garston Lock, a common tern divided into the canal immediately up-stream. Terns are quite numerous around the lake (only in summer, of course) and their aerial fishing displays are quite stunning. Much more exciting than the average K&A fisherman anyway.

The towpath now passes over a straight, dusty and gravelly roadway for about quarter of a mile. When the gravel road turns off left, the towpath carries straight on and up to the side of Sheffield Lock.

As part of the unrest mentioned at Burghfield, Sheffield Lock had its own excitement. The area had three mills - one for paper and two for corn. In 1725 one of the millers decided to drain the water from the canal through his mill gates: the canal was blocked for days. One bargeman had to unload most of his 50 tonnes of cargo in order to get through, another simply turned back. To add insult, both were stoned by mobs for their pains when they got to Reading.

Within a hundred yards of Sheffield Lock, the path crosses the minor Theale to Burghfield road at a swing bridge.

Theale can be reached by turning right and following the road for about half a mile over a railway bridge and straight on at a roundabout.

In Great Bath Road coaching days, Theale had the nickname of Little Soddom. How it got this name and precisely where BIG Soddom is, history doesn't record. With the coming of the motorway, a hypermarket (Savacentre) and numerous hi-tech looking industrial buildings, the village has turned into a suburb of Reading. Despite this, the recently renovated High Street has some charm and makes a welcome stopping place for lunch. The village has several pubs, a supermarket and various other small shops. Early closing is on Wednesday.

You can catch the train at Theale station west to Newbury and beyond, or east to Reading. There are also bus connections from the High Street. The BR station here is unmanned; you pay the conductor on the train. Don't forget that the platform nearest the canal is for trains going west (ie. to Newbury).

B. THEALE to WOOLHAMPTON

Distance:	6 miles/9½ kilometres
Map:	OS Landranger 175 (Reading & Windsor) and 174 (Newbury & Wantage)
Transport:	BR Reading (0734-595911)
	BR Theale, BR Aldermaston, BR Midgham (Woolhampton)
	NB: On Sundays trains stop at Theale & Thatcham but not at Aldermaston or Midgham (Woolhampton)
	Bee Line Buses (0734-581358) nos. 102 & 103 run half hourly between Reading and Newbury along A4 (Sundays every two to three hours)

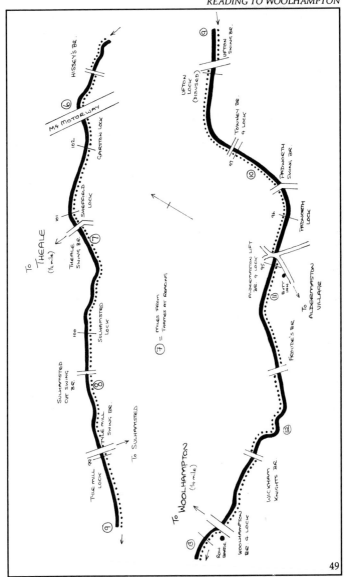

To THEALE
(½ mile)

HISSEY'S BR.

⑤

M4 MOTORWAY

102

GARSTON LOCK

101

SHEFFIELD LOCK

THEALE SWING BR.

⑦

100

SULHAMSTED LOCK

SULHAMSTED CUT SWING BR.

⑧

TYLE MILL SWING BR.

99

TYLE MILL LOCK

To SULHAMSTED

⑨

⑨ = MILES FROM THAMES AT READING

⑨

UFTON SWING BR.

UFTON LOCK (DISUSED)

97

TOWNEY BR. & LOCK

⑩

PADWORTH SWING BR.

96

PADWORTH LOCK

95

ALDERMASTON LIFT BR. & LOCK

BUTT INN

⑪

To ALDERMASTON VILLAGE

FROUDE'S BR.

⑫

WICKHAM KNIGHTS BR.

To WOOLHAMPTON
(¼ mile)

ROW BARGE

WOOLHAMPTON BR. & LOCK

⑬

49

Car Parks: Theale: On-road in town centre and near swing bridge.
Large station car park
Tyle Mill: On-road north of canal
Padworth: On-road north of canal
Aldermaston: Huge weekend car park just north of canal.
Some off-road south of canal
Woolhampton: On-road north of canal

If you are starting out from Theale BR station, make your way up to the road bridge that passes over the railway and turn left. Walk along the road (which bends firstly left and then right). Theale Swing Bridge will be found after about half a mile.

The second part of this section continues at the swing bridge by passing straight on over the minor road and along the southern, left-hand, bank of the canal. A signpost at the bridge informs us that this is part of the Lower Kennet Water Park and that Sulhamstead Swing Bridge is one mile upstream.

The building hidden behind the trees on the right is Sheffield Paper Mill, one of the mills discussed in the previous section.

A gravel pit with an intriguing conveyor belt system is now on the left. The path passes under a works bridge where a footpath (to Bottom Lane) goes off left. The K&A towpath carries straight on and curves around a series of lakes on the left called the Woolwich Green Lakes.

This peaceful and pleasant part of the walk is a good spot for birdlife. I've seen sedge and reed warblers here among the extensive reed beds. This time only a heron showed up. It sat looking somewhat bored with life, as walkers, fishermen and boats passed to and fro. On the canal itself, a single-parent family of swans looked up at passers by, hopeful of a cheap meal.

If you look back, across Cumber's Lake northwards to Theale, you get a good view of Holy Trinity Church. It's a fine building dating from the early 1800s. A local guidebook told me that it was built to a design based on Salisbury Cathedral. Maybe there are two Salisburys.

The River Kennet goes off right for a swift meander and weir whilst the canal continues on a new straight section called Sulhamstead Cut. Within a few yards we reach Sulhamstead Lock.

Sulhamstead Lock, along with Burghfield Lock, is the shortest on the canal at just seventy feet. This is mostly a result of the re-building which occurred in the 1960s, much of which was done by prisoners from Oxford gaol. It was found that it could be restored by building a new lock inside the old one and hence one of the largest locks became one of the smallest. The re-opening of the lock must have been quite a triumph - it had been closed from 1953 and was not navigable until 1968.

The big white house on the top of the hill to the left (south) is Sulhamstead House. Described as an 'ionic, porticoed house' (ie. the design was pinched from Greece and it's got columns), it was built in 1744. The grand days of splendour and money didn't last. In 1952 it became headquarters for the Berkshire Constabulary and latterly, in 1968, the Thames Valley police training school. Misdemeanours on this stretch should therefore be kept to a minimum (or at least out of view).

The route continues alongside some established ash trees to Sulhamstead Cut Swing Bridge where a footpath goes off left to Hazel Cottage (Bottom Lane). The way passes a weir to the right (where the Kennet leaves along its original path) and over a stile into an open field. Here the canal bends gracefully right and approaches Tyle Mill Lock. Before the lock a minor road crosses the canal at a swing bridge. Sulhamstead village is a few hundred yards to the left. There is some room for on-road parking to the north of the swing bridge.

If you turn right at the Tyle Mill Bridge you shortly (250 yards) come to the A4. On the corner there is now an upmarket fish and chip restaurant called Mulligans. This was until very recently the site of the pub 'Three Kings and Jack's Booth', a famous coaching inn. The pub was named (at least partly) after Jack of Newbury (variously known as John Winchcombe or John Smalwoode), said to be Newbury's most famous and wealthy son in the fifteenth century. Jack was a great cloth king and was often to be seen travelling along this portion of the road between Newbury and Reading and, presumably, drinking in this inn. He became so famous that Henry VIII, Catherine of Aragon and Cardinal Wolsey once came to visit him at his house in Northbrook Street in Newbury (whether they just sort of popped in on the off-chance or not isn't clear). Queen Elizabeth I later called on his son. Sadly Jack's name is no longer commemorated and this peculiar pub name is lost forever.

Tyle Mill itself is on the Kennet, a few hundred yards to the north. It was a large flour mill but burnt down in 1914. It was restored and used as a saw mill until about 1936. It's since been sold and is now used as a private house.

A signpost here suggests a circular walk to Aldermaston and Padworth. We, meanwhile, continue alongside the lock and on for about half a mile to Ufton. Here there is a small area for parking. A larger car park is labelled as being for fishermen only. The path now goes right across a newish concrete bridge, passes over the swing bridge and turns left to pass along the right-hand side of Ufton Lock. This section is well waymarked.

The river passing under the concrete bridge is in fact the Kennet which re-attaches itself to the canal here after a three mile period of separation to the south. The next section of the K&A, the Ufton New Cut, was built at the height of the canal's prosperity during the period 1830-35 and demonstrated the confidence of the management in its waterway just ten years before the arrival of the railway.

Ufton Lock has been degated. This isn't some sort of boarding school punishment, it actually means that the lock is no longer needed and its gates have been removed. Towney Lock (the next along) has been refurbished and the canal between here and there deepened. The relatively shallow rise/ fall of Ufton (one foot nine inches) became unnecessary and it was decided not to bother to undertake the expensive restoration.

Incidentally, if thirst has overtaken you, a pub can be found by turning right at the road and making your way up to the A4 (about quarter of a mile).

The towpath now bends gently left with the canal. Here there is the first of several pinch-points where the canal, the railway and the road come to within about 100 yards of each other.

Roads are pretty unloved things on the whole but their history is often fascinating. The name 'Great Bath Road' makes the A4 sound much nicer and suggests an interesting past - which indeed it does have. The road is actually not one of the many ancient or mediaeval routes but an eighteenth century development. At the time, the city of Bath was at the height of its fame as a spa and people flocked to visit it. To accommodate the flow of tourists from London, Parliament passed a series of turnpike bills so that funds could be gathered to build or refurbish the various sections of the road. The Reading to Puntfield (near Theale) section was one of the first in 1714. The section we're now on, Puntfield to Speenhamland (Newbury), got the go-ahead in 1728. If you think modern carriageway repairs go on forever you might wish to know that the Bath Road wasn't fully ready for a further fifty years or so. The Kennet Navigation was largely unaffected by the building of the road. Indeed, it took quite a lot of the heavy goods from it.

For interest, the London to Bath Royal Mail coach in the early nineteenth century had the following schedule: leave Brentford at 9.20pm, Reading 1.25am, Newbury 3.30am, Hungerford 4.40am and arrive Bath at 9.30am. The total journey was thus a fairly remarkable twelve hours.

We now pass the aforementioned Towney Lock and shortly afterwards reach Padworth Swing Bridge (re-built 1987). People using OS maps might be tempted by a 'PH' symbol marked on the A4. However, I'm afraid that that particular watering hole is now closed. The route passes a tatty works on our right (labelled on a canal navigation chart as an 'air liner fuel depot') and bends right. Within a short distance we reach Padworth Lock.

Padworth Lock is very neat and tidy. You almost feel that you shouldn't walk on it for fear of getting it dirty. The small gravestone on the other side of the lock is, in fact, a milestone. If you can't be bothered to visit it, it says 'Reading 11, Newbury 7¹/₂'. This is a bit awkward as both the navigation chart and I make it 10¹/₂· and 9. Rejecting the notion that continental drift has dragged the two places farther apart since the nineteenth century, I conclude that it probably depends on where you start and where you finish or even where the milestone was originally. In fact, the Act of Parliament which gave the go-ahead to the K&A required the canal company to erect milestones at half mile intervals all the way along. Despite this contradiction in terms, one wonders where all the others have gone.

Aldermaston wharf, lift bridge (carrying the A340 to Basingstoke) and lock are now just a hundred yards or so further on. The first signs of life are the British Waterways Board office on our right (with tourist information) and some Tudor-style buildings on our left. There is a large car park here at weekends (to the north of the canal and well-signposted). Some parking is also possible just to the south of the canal. The BR station can be found a hundred yards up the road by taking the left fork north (ie. to the right of the canal as we walk). Butt Inn can be found by turning left along the Basingstoke Road. It is about 200 yards on the right and does lunchtime bar snacks.

Aldermaston Lock is a work of art. It is a scheduled ancient monument and was beautifully restored in 1985. Constructed of brick, the chamber has

Aldermaston Lock

a series of delightful corrugations along the sides. Visitors are also treated to a fascinating information panel which describes both the lock and the area hereabouts.

Aldermaston Lock was originally called Brewery Lock as the buildings around it belonged to Strange's Brewery. In 1770 the brewery employed thirty men. The Strange family lived in the Tudor-looking house (called Bridge House) that we passed to our left just before the bridge. The building just before that was the malthouse. The buildings to the south of the lock contained the brewery itself. The enterprise closed in 1952. Readers of the information panel will learn even more!

The lift bridge, by the way, replaced an old wooden swing bridge in 1980. Those of a mischievous nature will be sad to learn that you need a special key to operate it. Even if you have the required tool, there are restrictions on its use at rush hour times.

Of course to most people Aldermaston is not famous for its brewery, lock or lift bridge. Most of us associate the name with the Atomic Weapons Research Establishment and the famous CND marches of the late 1950s. The first march (from London to Aldermaston) was in May 1958. Subsequent marches went the other way and concluded with a rally in London. Aldermaston attracted attention because nuclear warheads are designed here. They are then manufactured at the Royal Ordnance Factory at Burghfield (about one and a half miles south of the canal). The two sites were joined by a human chain of CND protesters on the highly appropriate April 1st, 1983. Neither site appears on current OS maps but AWRE is still here - about a mile or two to the south along the Basingstoke Road. There is little to see - unless you're a barbed wire connoisseur. A diversion is therefore not particularly recommended.

We now transfer our allegiance to the left bank and carry on along a section called the 'Salmon Cut' (presumably a misnomer). This passes the Sterling Greengate Cable Factory to the north and bends gently southwards. Straight rows of poplar trees have been planted in the fields to the south. The next bridge is Froude's Bridge - a brand new brick-built structure opened in August 1990. The new bridge replaced the old swing bridge.

Just after the cable factory we reach another pinch-point for the road, railway and canal. Unlike roads, railways are much loved by many people and, indeed, whole books have been written about this bit of line alone. For those disinclined to read an entire volume, the history of the line goes something like this. It was originally called the Berkshire and Hampshire Line and sanctioned by an Act of Parliament in 1845. The engineer was one Isambard Kingdom Brunel. Interestingly the materials brought in to construct the line were mostly transported on the K&A. A severe case of feeding the mouth that later bit. The line was opened (apparently without ceremony or celebration) four days before Christmas in 1847. Originally GWR broad gauge (7'0"), it was changed to standard gauge (4'8½") in 1874. The full route through to the south-west and the 'Cornish Riviera' was opened in 1906 and the express trains have been charging through ever since.

The Old Mill Hotel can be found by turning left at Froude's Bridge and heading towards Aldermaston. The Rising Sun public house is close by (half a mile) on the A4. To visit it turn right here and then left at the A4 T-junction. There is also a car park on the A4 in a large lay-by just beyond the Rising Sun pub (on the Newbury side).

After a short (quarter of a mile), fairly anonymous section of the canal (my notes say 'boring'), the way enters a beautiful section of willow trees and overgrown shrubbery. The canal winds one way and then the other and is alive with birds and, inevitably, fishermen.

At the end of the bends, the author was brought up sharp. Wickham Knights Swing Bridge has been replaced by a natty-looking footbridge. Unfortunately, this wasn't ready at the time of my walk. I was therefore forced to make a diversion north, over the railway line and out to the A4 where I turned left and walked by the side of the busy road into Woolhampton. You won't have to do that. You should therefore cross the bridge to the other bank to continue along a slightly straighter section and into Woolhampton.

From here on the canal has been subject to extensive repair. It was so derelict that it was impassable for many years and became known to boat owners as the 'Berkshire Gap'. Regular reports on the progress of restoration were published in the K&A Canal Trust magazine where, with the addiction of a soap opera, you could follow the developments lock by lock. It was with some celebration therefore that in July 1990 the first boats for many a year went from Reading to Newbury (and vice versa). Hopefully walkers will be able to as well soon.

This meandering section of the canal is called Woolhampton Water. The banks on the towpath side are strewn with wild hops which at the time of my walk were just ripening. Hops have separate sexes so it is only the female ones that bear the fruit with the characteristic papery scales. These are boiled with the mash to help clarify, flavour and even preserve the beer. Although the plant is native and wild in Britain, the preponderance of it in this area could suggest that it was once cultivated near here. Could it be related to Strange's Brewery perhaps?

If you are able to cross Wickam Knights Footbridge, you will shortly arrive at Woolhampton Swing Bridge and the Row Barge pub.

The swing bridge was being re-built when I passed along the

canal (another part of the Berkshire Gap). The minor road (Woolhampton to Brimpton) was completely blocked to cars although pedestrians were able to cross by means of a temporary footbridge. This situation should be rectified by the time you pass this way. The bridge apparently needed replacing fairly desperately. It's said that it took the author (and industrial archaeologist) Tom Rolt some three hours to open the old bridge in 1940 even with the help of a group of strong fellows. The new one will hopefully not prove so intransigent.

Woolhampton is a small place and an old Bath Road coaching village. Sadly, it is dominated by the A4. There is, however, more village to the north with a Victorian church, Woolhampton Park and Douai Abbey and School on the hill. Woolhampton Mill, situated between the railway and the canal, has been closed since 1930 but once was a good customer for the K&A, bringing grain to the mill and taking the flour, meal and other products away.

The Row Barge public house is situated next to the canal on the southern (left-hand) side. To reach the BR station, the A4 (for buses to Reading and Newbury), two more pubs and a small shop, turn right to go into Woolhampton (200 yards).

By the way, if you're coming by train and ask for Woolhampton you may get a confused look. The station here is called Midgham after a village a couple of miles up the road. I am assured that this is because GWR thought that the station would get confused with Wolverhampton. No, I didn't believe it either. Again, the station is unmanned so you pay on the train. On Sundays it's also 'unpassengered' as the trains do not stop here at all. If you're doing this section on a Sunday, and wish to return to car or accommodation, you should check the bus timetable or walk on to Thatcham (three miles).

3: THE K&A WALK
WOOLHAMPTON to HUNGERFORD

We are now entering the far western reaches of Royal Berkshire in a walk that's scrubby at first but which improves no end. Initially the way passes through some tatty, industrialised areas around Colthrop and Thatcham. Luckily this is quickly followed by some pleasant country, rich in bird and insect life. By lunchtime, we reach the highly agreeable bustling town of Newbury. From there, we seem to leave the twentieth century behind and the path enters some wonderful walking country to pass through the village of Kintbury before reaching Hungerford.

The canal in the first part of this section was, until recently completely blocked to through traffic. Recent and current renovation is to be seen all the way along. At Newbury the Kennet Navigation ends; this was once the limit to barges from the Thames. The K&A canal of 1810 starts here.

As in the first section, the canal runs close to the A4 and the BR Reading-Hungerford line throughout. Trains stop at Woolhampton (Midgham), Thatcham, Newbury, Kintbury and Hungerford, permitting a reasonable choice of starting and stopping points (unless it's a Sunday). Beyond Newbury buses become a very scarce commodity indeed.

Newbury is a good shopping centre. Thatcham and Hungerford have a small selection of shops. Woolhampton and Kintbury have small village shops. There are pubs at various points all the way along.

A. WOOLHAMPTON to NEWBURY

Distance:	6½ miles / 11 kilometres
Map:	OS Landranger 174 (Newbury & Wantage)
Transport:	BR Reading & Newbury (0734-595911)
	Un- (or partially) manned BR stations at Midgham (closed Sundays) and Thatcham
	Bee Line Buses (0635-40743) run Newbury to Reading (see section 1)
Car Parks:	Woolhampton: On-road and station car park
	Thatcham: Parking at and near station (next to canal)
	Newbury: Extensive in-town - notably at Newbury Wharf next to canal
Tourist Info:	Newbury on 0635-30267

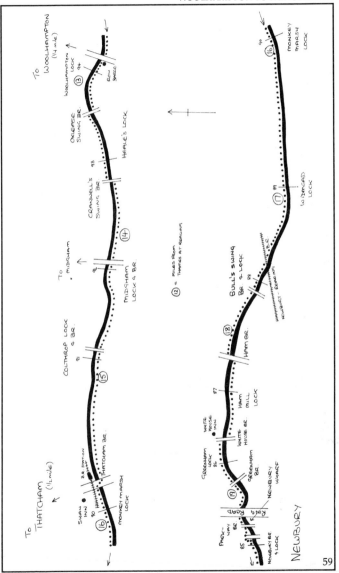

To WOOLHAMPTON (¼ mile)

WOOLHAMPTON LOCK 9ft ⑬
ROW SWING

OXLEASE SWING BR.

HEALE'S LOCK

CRANWELL'S SWING BR. 93

⑭

To MIDGHAM

MIDGHAM LOCK & BR. 92

COLTHROP LOCK & BR. 91

⑮

THATCHAM BR.

To THATCHAM (½ mile)

SWAN INN
R.R. STATION
MONKEY MARSH LOCK 90

⑯

⑫ = MILES FROM THAMES AT READING

MONKEY MARSH LOCK

⑯ 90

WIDMEAD LOCK 89 ⑰

BULL'S SWING BR. & LOCK 88

NEWBURY – REBACK

⑱

HAM BR.

HAM MILL LOCK 87

WHITE HOUSE INN

WHITE HOUSE BR.

GREENHAM LOCK 86

GREENHAM BR.

NEWBURY WHARFE

⑲

KING'S ROAD BR.

PARK WAY BR. 85

NEWBURY BR. & LOCK

NEWBURY

59

If you have started this section from Woolhampton centre, you should proceed south on the Woolhampton to Brimpton Road that starts almost opposite the Angel Inn on the A4. From Midgham station turn right down the minor road. In both cases, the canal will be found immediately before the Row Barge Inn at Woolhampton Bridge. To get to Newbury, cross the canal and turn right.

From the Row Barge, the walk takes the southern bank and within just a few yards reaches Woolhampton Lock. The precise route for the next mile will change over the coming years as swing bridges are replaced or re-built. When the author walked this section, a number of scaffolding bridges were in position while repairs were made. In essence, the path crosses to the northern bank at the next swing bridge (Oxlease) and then back to the southern bank at the following swing bridge (Cranwell's). In between the two is Heale's Lock.

All this to-ing and fro-ing keeps the mind amused through some relatively uninteresting countryside. Midgham Church on the hill to the right (north) represents the only bit of sight-seeing for a while and should be made the most of.

In 1892 it was suggested that a reservoir be built here to supply water to London. The lake would have covered the entire area from Newbury to Aldermaston and would have submerged the villages of Aldermaston and Woolhampton as well as the Bath Road, the railway and the canal. The road and railway would have had to have been diverted by over ten miles and presumably, the canal would have been abandoned. There were one or two objections and you may have guessed that the idea was dropped. The proposed topic of conversation between here and Thatcham then is whether the reservoir would have improved the scenery or not. (Interestingly a similar scheme was suggested in the 1940s. This time it was slightly to the south along the Enborne Valley from Brimpton to Newtown in south Newbury).

Midgham would have been more busy than it is if the plan of 1824 had been enacted. In it, the Basingstoke Canal was to be joined to the K&A by the Hants and Berks Junction Canal (Old Basing to Midgham). The intention was to find a viable alternative to the Thames which was often unnavigable in parts and halted traffic at certain times of the year. The K&A Canal Company was in favour of the link but the Thames Commissioners were not and fought the idea with some vigour. By 1827 the

Thames had won the day despite three presentations to Parliament. The idea was never revived.

The route crosses the Midgham to Brimpton road and carries on to Midgham Lock. Turn right at the road if you want to visit the Coach & Horses pub on the A4 (400 yards). The Reading-Newbury buses also stop there. A notice on Midgham Lock explains that it was re-built using money from a TV company.

Dredging of the canal has resulted in the towpath being covered in a thick layer of mud. In a dry September the path was passable but in winter this section could be very difficult indeed. Walkers may need to descend left to avoid the worst parts of the mire.

The towpath goes over a stile and onto a more pleasant path. Ahead the huge edifice of a factory looms. The path passes over a weir (Hitchman's Ditch) and then quickly becomes embroiled in industrial workings. There is now an old sewage works to the left and extensive warehousing to the right. Keep to the small track close to the canal which passes some boarded-up housing on the left.

Colthrop was the site of two grist (corn) mills and a paper mill in mediaeval times. One of the grist mills became a fulling mill in 1540. In 1805 a Frenchman called Fourdrinier came to live in Colthrop and converted the fulling mill into a paper mill based on his own design of paper-making machinery. His invention permitted continuous paper or board manufacture and the principle is still used today. The pulp is poured onto a continuously moving drum or belt where it not only forms the cellulose mat but also dries. This invention effectively turned what was then a craft into an industrial process.

This site has been a major paper and board works ever since and is now part of the Reed Paper Group. At one time 100,000 tonnes of packaging board were made here every year. Those returning by train will be able to see the great stacks of old newspapers that await recycling. The whole site covers 160 acres and is being redeveloped. Many other companies now occupy space here. In fact, this whole area between Reading and Newbury is called the British Silicon Valley and is currently enjoying great prosperity. The growth of hi-tech industry is reputedly a result of its proximity to the M4 and Heathrow airport.

Despite the above (or perhaps because of the above), this is my least favourite part of the Berkshire section of the walk. It's messy and unattractive and seems to last forever. For those reading this at the beginning of it, I can tell you that it actually only lasts about a mile or so and that you will be rewarded in heaven (which begins after Newbury). Maybe the redevelopment will brighten it up a bit - it could do with it.

Just to prove that appearances can be deceptive; amidst the gloom and industrial dereliction, a kingfisher darted from the undergrowth and shot off towards the board factory. It was the first of ten spotted on the entire walk.

The end of the Colthrop section is marked by the appearance of a farmhouse on the left (Rainsford Farm) and Thatcham station over on the other side of the canal. Here is Thatcham Bridge which carries an increasingly important road from the A4 down in the direction of Basingstoke and Southampton. There are car parking places here next to the station.

There's no doubt that BR deserves a mention for the stations along this line. They have all been re-built to a neat design and the paintwork is a cheerful bright red. Thatcham is no exception. The station here is manned in the mornings and has an automatic ticket machine. Most trains stop here - even on Sundays - and so it can make a useful spot to walk to or from.

Thatcham is one of the prime growth areas of the Thames valley and examples of the new development can be seen by standing on Thatcham Bridge and peering north. New housing and industrial developments abound and what was once a small village is now virtually a new town.

Despite the view from the bridge, the place does have a history. Before the conquest Thatcham was a prosperous cloth town and had a close rivalry with its near neighbour Newbury. In the early twelfth century, Newbury men were known to attack the Thatcham market by upturning stalls and scaring the locals. Henry II reconfirmed his support for the Thatcham market and issued three charters, one of which compelled the men of the village to attend the market on Sundays or receive a £10 fine! This action appeared to work and things calmed down a bit. However, by 1500, Newbury clearly had the upper hand and became one of the principal cloth towns in southern England while Thatcham declined, with the help of the Black Death, into a small satellite village.

If you arrive at the right time, the Swan Inn is visible from the canal on the right-hand (northern) side. There are more shops and places to eat in town (three quarters of a mile) as well as access to the bus service. Turn right at the bridge, cross the railway and take the left-hand fork at the roundabout. There is a car park in the centre of town. Early closing is Wednesday. Newbury is now four miles away.

The towpath now crosses sides and proceeds on the northern (right-hand) bank. The route is waymarked at Thatcham Bridge to Ham Lock (on the outskirts of Newbury). After 150 yards of broad gravel track we reach Monkey Marsh Lock.

Monkey Marsh was still being worked on as I made my way along here. I had to duck into the hedge to avoid a cement lorry that careered by and out into the Thatcham road. A group of men was spreading the concrete to make up the mooring site to the east of the lock. The lock itself was operational though still bedecked with scaffolding.

Like Garston Lock, Monkey Marsh is a turf-sided lock and a listed ancient monument. Turf-sided locks are not completely turf-sided. Normally half the height of the internal chamber is made of brick or stone or wood and only the top half is soil (covered in turf) angled at about 45°. They were made this way basically because they were cheaper to build. As water flows in from upstream, the turf is flooded. In normal use, it is stable enough to retain the water until the upper gates are closed and the internal level returned to the downstream height. In wet weather the system works well, although in drought a lot of water is absorbed by the turf banks. This means that filling the lock can take much longer than a normal-sided chamber and that water loss from the system as a whole is much greater. The stretch of canal between Reading and Newbury has never been short of water so although normal-sided locks are preferred these days, these turf-siders can still survive as operational locks without disturbing the system too much. In general though, turf-sided locks are now very rare on the British canal system.

The compound to the right is a Ministry of Defence establishment and hence cannot be spoken of (mostly because I know nothing about it).

The improving landscape now passes Monkey Marsh Swing Bridge and along Long Cut. The path here is narrow and overgrown and continues for just under a mile to Widmead Lock.

After Colthrop this section is very pleasant. In September the hedges were heavy with blackberries and elderberries, and the canal seemed to be left just to me and the coots. At least I thought so until a canoeist swished past at almost break-neck speed.

The canal is a popular place for canoeing and has an annual race. It all began in 1948 when someone from Pewsey offered £20 to anybody able to go from the town to Westminster in under one hundred hours. The idea bombed in Pewsey but was rapidly taken up by the people of Devizes. The local scouts promptly covered the 125 miles between the town and London in just under ninety hours. Since then it's become an annual event and the times have come down dramatically. The record time is now in the region of sixteen hours! The race is always held at Easter, crews leaving Devizes on Good Friday morning.

After the lock, the path widens and has been laid with gravel (from south Reading perhaps?) A sign says that the fishing rights are now owned by Newbury Angling Association and we are within three miles of the town. We pass a series of lakes with abundant reed growth on our right and, beyond a fine stand of graceful willow trees, a lake with about fifty coots on our left. The path contracts and we pass to the left of a pill box into undergrowth.

The K&A, with its abundant small lakes and ponds, is an excellent place for dragonflies and the air around this particular spot seemed to be black with them. Dragonflies are probably one of the easiest groups of insects to recognise with their long, slim bodies, broad cellophane-like wings and massive, all-embracing eyes. There are forty-odd different types in this country; broadly divided into the large, 'true' dragonflies and the slightly smaller and more delicate damselflies. A common damselfly which is easy to see here is a blue-green one about two inches long with blob-like blue patches on its wings. This is the banded demoiselle. Like all dragonflies, the young insect spends two years underwater as a nymph before emerging into the air as a proud and elegant damselfly. The adult earns a living by catching small insects in flight and this they do with remarkable agility. Dragonflies can fly forwards, backwards, sideways and upside-down; they even glide. If you see two looped together this is because courting couples do so in flight, with the male grasping his true love's neck with his tail claspers. This can produce the peculiar circular dragonfly that can often be seen flitting around your head in a seemingly random and uncontrolled fashion. Probably best to keep your head down until the path opens out a bit.

The towpath passes under the Reading-Newbury railway bridge (note how the old bridge supports don't touch the newer bridge) and out, across a small bridge and on to Bull's Lock. The way then continues with the canal to our left and a river (which eventually

Hissey's Bridge, Theale

leads to the River Lambourn) to our right. After one hundred yards a swing bridge passes over the canal. The path carries straight on.

I had planned at this point to show you the delights of Newbury Racecourse but all we can see from here (to our left and directly south) is the railway and a motley collection of warehouses. You'll just have to wait to get a good view from the train.

The path crosses a weir bridge and passes onto a road bridge. Here we climb up to the road and cross to the other bank. To our left new hi-tech, red-coloured, air-conditioned offices contrast nicely with the barn-conversion offices to our right. The towpath crosses the rickety-looking metal bridge and down to an overgrown path which leads through some buddleia bushes to Ham Mill Lock.

Graffiti on the lock informed me that someone had made love there on the first of August 1990. But why? I can only think that it must be more romantic in the dark. It didn't have a lot to commend it during the day - unless you like a view of a DIY superstore. Still, if you continue on a few yards and look back right up the weir stream, you can see the rather dilapidated remnants of Ham Mill. Quite nice in itself but with the additional claim of once being the home of one John Hore. Who? I hear you asking.

You have been treading all over one of John Hore's achievements for the last eighteen and a half miles. John Hore was appointed as engineer and surveyor for the Kennet Navigation in 1718 at the princely salary of £60 per annum (plus expenses!) He'd been appointed to make good some earlier rather disastrous attempts at canal building, to shorten the route somewhat and to finish it off. He did pretty well, the canal is only one mile longer than the road. He was also responsible for the twenty locks which have brought us 134 foot higher than we were in Reading. He was obviously a success because the Avon Navigation (that part of the canal between Hanham and Bath) appointed him as its engineer in 1724.

His engineering skills must obviously have outstripped his financial acumen. It's said that he spent some of his own money during the building of the canal but failed to keep receipts and was unable to account for some quite large sums. The Kennet Navigation Company refused to pay him and by the 1730s he became quite destitute. Luckily fate, in the shape of some much needed engineering work, took a hand and Kennet Navigation re-employed him to organise it. He had a higher salary and a company horse.

Crane at Newbury Wharfe

On the latter point, history does not tell us whether he had a choice of colours.

Ham achieved a dubious reputation at the time of the Kennet Navigation when the local landowner, Lord Dysart, decided that a good way of raising cash was to charge his own toll on canal users. He asked for 3d (three old pennies, for younger readers, is a sum equivalent to just over 1p) for every horse that passed. The Navigation Company took the matter to court and won. However, the barge masters were asked for an annual subscription towards fighting such cases in the future.

The path and canal now bend left, then right and pass over a weir. This, according to the notice, is another drowning black spot.

Seeing this sign reminded me of the similar one just after Southcote. The difference being that this time there were no fishermen to be seen. In fact, I hadn't seen any since Woolhampton. It's funny how you don't miss them when they're not there.

The route now follows the smell of beefburgers over a footbridge to a roadside restaurant. The White House public house is here on the right. We turn left. Here the path passes the only remaining buttress of a railway bridge.

This was the Didcot, Newbury & Southampton Railway and formed part of Newbury's plan to become the railway hub of central-southern England. Perhaps the augurs were out when Lord & Lady Carnavon (from nearby Highclere Castle) opened the line in August 1879 in the pouring rain. Passenger services stopped in 1960 and the line was eventually lifted in 1967. When I was passing, a water-colour painter had set up his easel to record this last tombstone for posterity.

We are now very close to Newbury centre. Within a short distance, the path arrives at a cutting to our right which houses the Greenham Boat Company. We pass over the footbridge and bear right to Greenham Lock.

If you're hopping around wondering where you've heard of Greenham before, hop no longer. Greenham rose to international fame in the early 1980s when Cruise missiles and peace women descended on the local NATO Greenham Common Airfield (about one and a half miles south-east of Greenham Lock). Whether the notoriety came from the missiles or the women depends on your point of view but either or both made Newbury, and Greenham, famous around the world.

The path now heads quickly off towards central Newbury by

passing over a weir and near some admirably kept allotments to our right. There are some boat mooring spaces to the left. A path to the Newbury Town Football Club ground tempts fans to the right.

Off left on the Kennet proper (ie. not the canal) is the site of Greenham Mill. An event here in 1811 shot the town to national attention and has given guide book writers something to fill their volumes with ever since. Sir John Throckmorton wagered £1,000 that wool clipped from sheep at sunrise could be made into a coat by sunset. Mr Coxeton, the mill owner, wove the cloth and Mr White, a local tailor, cut it. Nine men were involved in the sewing. The wager was won with hours to spare. Animal lovers should not read the next bit - the sheep involved were slaughtered and roasted for a general town celebration in the evening.

The mill itself continued to have an interesting time. It was firstly converted to flour milling and for some years supplied a special flour to Huntley & Palmer in Reading. It was then sold in 1903 and used as a power station.

Just where the canal broadens dramatically, the A34 road bridge crosses. The K&A towpath carries straight on but a detour into Newbury is recommended and completes this section of the walk. To avoid having to cross the A34, go under the bridge and take the steps up from there. Cross the canal and take the steps down right to Newbury Wharf.

You are now in Newbury! Well done! Nineteen miles from the Thames, just over ninety from London and still seventy-four to Bristol. You might be interested to know that the time taken for boats to navigate from Reading was usually one day unless they stopped en route. A marathon runner might do it in under two hours. Oh well.

Newbury Wharf is now a car park and popular lunching spot for office workers. It was once the terminus for the Kennet Navigation and was as far as narrow boats and barges could go from 1723 until the opening of the Newbury to Kintbury portion of the K&A in 1797. The wharf here was therefore an important unloading site for goods from London (coal, timber, rope, tar, iron, groceries and heavy goods) and loading site for goods to London (mostly farm produce from all over the western parts of Berkshire into Wiltshire).

This site was originally that of Newbury Castle which, after being stormed by King Stephen and seized by King John, fell into disrepair. After a brief renaissance as a workshop in the seventeenth century, the site was purchased by the Kennet Navigation Company in 1723 and converted to a wharf.

In the centre portion of the wharf (where the cars now are) there was once a harbour area where boats could load and unload. This was filled in during the 1920s when the council bought the wharf and converted it to its present use. The stone building to the right, now leased to the K&A Canal Trust, is said to have been built out of bits of the old castle. The rather splendid long, low, balconied granary dates from the opening of the Kennet Navigation and now houses a cafe, some shops, the tourist information office and the local museum.

The museum has a collection of old photographs of the wharf and canal at Newbury. It also has displays on the town's former cloth industry, and a section on hot-air ballooning as well as some fascinating items on the Civil War and some less appealing stuffed birds.

In 1790 vast crowds from up to a hundred miles away flocked to the wharf to see a prize fight which was to be held on a kind of floating stage in the basin. The authorities didn't approve. They stopped the entertainment and arrested both prospective pugilists. They were, however, soon released and continued their punch up elsewhere.

Two battles and a skirmish of a more serious nature occurred at Newbury during the Civil War. The battles did not go well for the cavaliers (the royalists) who lost both; the first at Wash Common to the south (where large burial mounds can still be seen) and the second to the north at Donnington Castle. Both sites are within walking distance if you wish to visit them. (Ask for directions at the tourist office).

By the turn of the nineteenth century, Newbury's cloth trade was in decline and the town had to make the most of its confluence of north-south, east-west road, rail and canal routes. It also started to develop a name for hunting and racing. Sporting gentlemen were brought here from London at ten shillings a time to indulge in some outdoor pastimes. Latterly, the town has prospered with new industries and the revitalised airbase. It is also well within commuting distance of London despite its country town atmosphere.

There are two cafes and a pub on or near the wharf. If neither prove satisfactory or provisions are needed, the centre of Newbury can be found by passing the museum and continuing along Wharf Street. Turning left or right here will lead to a wide range of shops and eating places. Market day is Thursday, early closing Wednesday. Public conveniences and the *good-size car park are situated on the wharf. The bus station is along Wharf Street and left. The BR station is in the same direction except that you continue along Cheap Street and turn right at the end.*

B. NEWBURY to HUNGERFORD

Distance:	8¹/2 miles/14 kilometres
Map:	OS Landranger 174 (Newbury & Wantage)
Transport:	BR Newbury, enquiries to Reading (0734-595911)
	Un- (or partially) manned BR stations at Kintbury and Hungerford
	Bee Line & Thamesdown Buses (0635-40743) run Newbury to Hungerford but infrequently
Car Parks:	Newbury: Extensive town parking - notably at Newbury Wharf next to canal
	Marsh Benham: Small amount on-road
	Kintbury: Small area near station
	Hungerford: Town centre near station

The second part of this section starts at the Newbury wharf. We have to return to the far bank to rejoin the towpath. Instead of going via the A34 road bridge, take the small road that runs to the left of the K&A Canal Trust building. This crosses the canal. At the end of the bridge, bear right down some steps into the park. Turn right and then right again to continue the walk. The path winds for a short distance behind some buildings until Newbury Bridge is reached. Bear right up a small passage to Northbrook Street. Cross the road and enter another small street directly opposite. At the end, turn left (going straight on takes you into a cafe) and pass through an enclosed passageway. This returns you to the canal. Turn right (you actually have no choice unless a keen swimmer) and walk over a small footbridge and up to Newbury Lock.

It is perhaps worth noting that Thomas Hardy called Newbury Kennetbridge, and presumably this was it. The current Newbury Bridge was built in 1770 and replaced a series of wooden ones which either fell down or were washed away in floods. As the canal stopped at Newbury at that time, there is no towpath here. This might be mildly awkward for walkers but must have been annoying for bargemen wanting to go

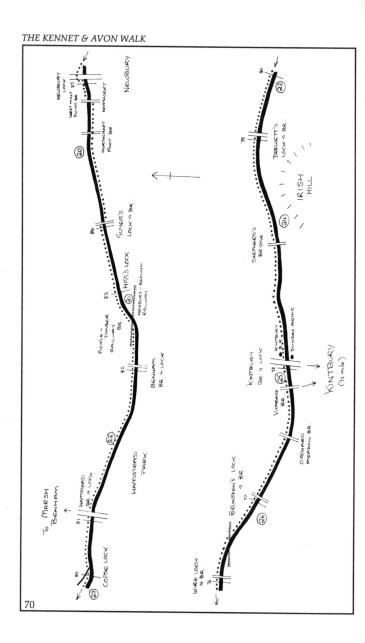

NEWBURY LOCK
WEST MILLS SWING BR.
NORTHCROFT
NEWBURY
NORTHCROFT FOOT BR.
20
85
GUYER'S LOCK & BR.
84
HIGG'S LOCK
21
83
PICKLE-TIMBER RAILWAY BR.
NEWBURY-BEDWIN RAILWAY
BENHAM BR. & LOCK
82
19
HAMSTEAD PARK
HAMSTEAD BR. & LOCK
81
TO MARSH BENHAM
COPSE LOCK
80
23

DRUETT'S LOCK & BR.
79
23
80
IRISH HILL
24
SHEPHERD'S BRIDGE
KINTBURY LOCK
79½
KINTBURY BR. & LOCK
78½
DUNDAS ARMS
25
KINTBURY (½ mile)
VICARAGE BR.
78
ORCHARD MEADOW BR.
BRUNSDEN'S LOCK & BR.
77
26
WIRE LOCK & BR.
74

upstream. Downstream traffic could just flow with the waters. Upstream traffic had more problems. The first step was to tie the boat to the bank just below the bridge. The horse was then led through the route that we've just come along. At the lock, a tow-line was attached to a float and thrown into the canal. The current took the float downstream and under the bridge where it was fished out by the bargeman. The rope was attached to the barge and the horse was able to tow the vessel under the bridge. A similar method was used at Brewery Gut in Reading. If you look carefully at the corner of the towpath wall, you should be able to see the grooves worn by the hauling lines.

Now that we are up to Newbury Lock, we are on the K&A proper. This section was opened in 1797 (the lock in 1796) and the full route to Bath was completed in 1810. The length of the new canal was fifty-six miles and could be covered in just three days nine hours. Will it take us that long? Will we make it at all?

If you enjoy bustle and traffic, you should halt a while at Newbury Lock and look back. We are in for a period of relative peace and tranquillity and you may miss the noise. Certainly Newbury seems to have changed somewhat since L.Salmon wrote in his travelogue of Berkshire in 1913: "The little town of Newbury wakes up once a week...upon market day... This spasmodic weekly movement being over, the little town for another seven days appears to doze again." Newbury obviously wasn't much then but it does appear to have had an eight day week.

The ruin on the right of the lock, by the way, was once the lock keeper's cottage and was lived in until 1958.

The broad, popular path takes us down to West Mills Street; a picturesque and historic part of old Newbury. Next to a tall, converted mill building (the silo of West Mill), we cross the canal on the swing bridge and turn right. The path now speeds us out of town.

Town and West Mills were both bought by Hovis in 1939. Town Mill (knocked down in the name of progress in the 1970s) produced flour for the famous little brown loaves. West Mill produced animal feed. The main part of West Mill burnt down whilst employed as a furniture store in the 1960s.

The buildings on the left-hand side are the weavers' cottages. These seventeenth century buildings were once weaving houses. They were later converted into accommodation for canal builders and are now private houses.

To the north of the canal, Newbury quickly disappears as we pass Northcroft Recreation Centre. Victorian houses with long, keenly attended gardens are to the south.

At the point where a stream enters the canal on the northern (right-hand) bank, a little grebe appeared from nowhere and bobbed up and down on the water. I'd not seen one as close as this before. Dabchicks, as they are often called, are usually extremely shy and tend to dive as soon as you raise your binoculars. This one was so close I didn't need them. The nest is interesting in that it's composed of a floating pile of rotting vegetation that acts like an old-fashioned garden hot bed. As the plant material breaks down, it warms up - just like a hot bed or a compost heap - and helps the birds incubate their eggs.

The towpath is now bordered to the left with relatively new housing. After about 150 yards, the remains of a railway bridge is on the right-hand, northern, bank of the canal.

This is all that's left of the Lambourn line's railway bridge. The line, opened in 1898 and closed in 1973, ran from Newbury up to the famous horse-racing village of Lambourn, high on the downs. The bridge was the scene of a tragedy in the very first week of the line opening. Two boys, playing on the bridge, watched a boat go underneath and then got up to rush to the other side to watch it reappear. Tragically, a passing train, travelling at just ten miles per hour, killed both of them.

The path now passes through some quiet and relaxing countryside. We pass two houses on our left and a brick-built bridge over the canal. We cross here and pass Guyer's lock which is now on our left.

Both the bridge and the lock are named after a royalist troop commander in the first Battle of Newbury. The name of the next lock, Higg's Lock, is similarly derived.

Herbalists and organic gardeners might be found congregating along this stretch as the area between the two locks is particularly rich in comfrey. If you believe the scribes, comfrey can be used for virtually everything. Comfrey ointments are reckoned to be just about the best skin cream in existence, the tea alleviates rheumatism and arthritis, tablets cure internal complaints, powder is used as a poultice and gardeners use it as a fertilizer. With all these uses, it's surprising there's so much about.

After Higg's Lock, the path passes under a railway bridge (the Newbury-Bedwyn line 'Pickletimber' bridge). Here high reeds temporarily hide the canal from view. Take the path under the bridge (Benham Bridge) and up to Benham Lock. There now follows a straight stretch which includes a concrete path over a weir. This is the Kennet, which then immediately runs off south.

This is a beautiful part of the canal and may remind you of the gardens of a stately home. The reason for this is that it is - in a way. The area to our left (the south side of the canal) is Hamstead Park and this particular piece of water is called Benham Broad. The original landowner here, Lord Craven, was also one of the canal's promoters. He insisted that the company prettify his stretch rather than make it into a simple stark canal. And a jolly good job they did too! In fact, this part of the K&A became quite popular for outings from Newbury - even into the twentieth century; Newbury Sunday school outings, for example, were held here just before the First World War.

Immediately south of Benham Lock is the small village of Enborne. I wouldn't pass comment on the place at all if it wasn't for an intriguing reference in J.E.Vincent's 1919 guide to the area Highways and Byways in Berkshire. *Here he says that Enborne is 'remarkable mainly for a "custom" hard to match for ribald obscenity even in mediaeval times'. But he doesn't say what it was!*

It is now just a short walk to Hamstead Bridge and Lock at Marsh Benham. Here a minor road (A4-Hamstead Marshall) crosses the canal.

This is a nice spot with 'Country Life' houses. It's hard to see but there is a church on the hill to the south. The basis is late Norman with fourteenth and eighteenth century additions.

Car parking may be possible here but it would be on the road and tight. The Red House Inn can be found by turning right and then first right (about 400 yards). Kintbury, the next opportunity to stop, is two and a half miles away.

The path now passes a weir to the left and some heavily pollarded willows in a low meadow to the right. The next lock is within half a mile. Just before it the Kennet flows in from the right. We cross it over a sturdy metal bridge.

The Kennet's appearance reminded me a lot of certain parts of the Test in Hampshire. This stretch is firmly labelled as part of the Morewood Estate and strictly private.

Before I forget, the lock is Copse Lock.

After the point where Benham Broad water leaves the canal on the south bank (left), the path passes alongside a thick hawthorn hedge. On the other side of the hedge is the Kennet and the 'Three Arches' overspill (plus about fiftyCanada geese!). Streams leave to the right (the Kennet) and to the left (Peartree Brook). The route passes to the right-hand side of Drewett's Bridge and Lock and on with some boggy, low-lying land on the right. After a couple of hundred yards, the railway line almost runs into the canal but then backs off.

The wooded hill to the left is Irish Hill. Believe it or not this rural scene was once a hive of industry and mining works. Here whiting was quarried. You thought a whiting was a fish, right? Well, whiting is also a type of chalk that was used in the paint industry. At Irish Hill, the soft, upper layer of chalk was scooped off and ground before being settled out in tanks. The resulting slurry was dried and then shipped to Bristol on the canal. This activity ceased at the turn of this century and was finally wound up in the 1930s. Zinc oxide and titanium dioxide are now used to make paint extra-super-white.

At the bridge a footpath notice points left for those wishing to investigate Irish Hill. The towpath continues on the northern bank of the canal. A pill box with a 1960s style picture-window is passed in a field on the right. The first signs of Kintbury should soon be detectable by eye and by nose (the sewage works is on the southern side of the canal). The fishing is now Kintbury AC. The path continues on gravel between the canal and a tributary of the Kennet (the main stream is about 600 yards further north). We pass over a concrete bridge with a stream off right. The path passes to the left of a house and into Kintbury.

This could be a major stopping point if you feel like a break. The station should be obvious to you on the right. Again it is unmanned and the trains to Hungerford/Bedwyn are on the canal side of the station. Public conveniences are very convenient being right next to the canal. Turn left for other services. There are three pubs in town; the Dundas Arms is just here on the southern side of the canal; the Prince of Wales can be found by turning left and left again (200-300 yards) and the Blue Ball farther still by turning left and keeping going ı or about 600 yards. The town centre has a couple of small shops and a cafe - again turn left and follow the road for about 400 yards. There is a small amount of parking next to the railway station. Hungerford is three miles away.

Kintbury's association with the canal is quite intimate because the first chairman of the K&A company, Charles Dundas MP (later Baron Amesbury) lived here at Barton Court. He was a great supporter of the enterprise and saw it through many of its early difficulties into a going concern. He died in 1832 from cholera and therefore, perhaps thankfully, missed the canal's decline after the GWR was built. There is a tablet commemorating his memory in the small, neat church near the centre of the village.

As he was the chairman, it was rather appropriate that Kintbury to Newbury (five and a half miles) was the first section of the canal proper to be officially opened in June 1797. The day was full of pomp and ceremony. The band of the Dragoons sailed up the canal on a barge and was met by Dundas and the other company directors. The journey took two and a half hours. Everybody then had a grand lunch. For unexplained reasons the journey back took three and a half hours.

During its operational life, the Kintbury wharf was a busy one, unloading coke and iron from south Wales (there was a local ironworks here) and exporting agricultural machinery, bricks, silk and wool goods, as well as whiting, of course. Nowadays the wharf is used solely for mooring of private boats and for launching excursion trips. When I was here a party of old age pensioners was boarding the Kennet Boat Company's barge for an outing. The boats are hauled by a sturdy shire horse who with just a few paces has the barge belting along at a fair lick and completely noiselessly - apart, that is, from the chattering OAPs. If you think that this is a bit hard on the poor old horse, it is perhaps worth pointing out that hauling barges is considerably easier than hauling road wagons. It's said that whereas two tons can be pulled by a horse on a road, some fifty to one hundred tons can be towed on a barge.

The agricultural machinery business brought the village to a wider notice in the 1830s. The introduction of 'modern' tools led to riots and outbreaks of vandalism. The rioters must have been reasonably well organised as it is said that the Blue Ball pub was used as their headquarters. A detachment of the Grenadier Guards was sent to calm things down and eventually one person was executed, several deported and many others imprisoned. Otherwise, it seemed like a quiet, peaceful place to me.

The path continues along the northern side of the canal and under a bridge.

This short stretch (about one hundred yards) must have enough horseradish along it to supply the whole of the country. The bridge can take you to the church (St. Mary's) and then into town should you want to go (turn left). If you go up to the bridge and turn right, a public footpath eventually leads to the A4 but passes quite close to Barton Court.

The canal path passes some impressive houses on the left and then bends right, to pass over a stream and on into more peaceful countryside. The next bridge is Orchard Meadow Bridge and, despite an electricity sub-station, can be enjoyed using a seat immediately before it. Pass under the bridge and along a straight section with the railway close to the right-hand side. At the next bridge we rise up to the right and then down to Brunsden's Lock. The path then continues to go under the railway bridge.

Even in September after a dry summer this section was muddy. Walkers planning to pass this way in winter or early spring might wish to prepare themselves suitably. The reason for the mud was that the level of the path was only a couple of inches above the level of the canal water.

The ravages of the gales of 1987 and 1990 can be seen along this stretch. Beech trees have been up-ended and willows severely, and not attractively, pruned or pushed off the upright.

The path now opens out to a broad, grassy track and then onto a small metalled road. This takes us up to Wirelock Bridge and Lock.

The rumble of traffic that can be heard here from the north (right) is the A4. I'm afraid it stays with us until Froxfield, a short distance after Hungerford.

The path goes back to being a broad, grassy track and bends gently left. We pass through a gate (or over a stile) and into a field.

This field is a beautiful spot. The Kennet is close to us on the right and there are numerous seats planted all along. Romantics should take advantage of the seats because we are about to say goodbye to the Kennet. It now turns slightly north-west (it rises just south of Swindon then passes through Avebury and Marlborough) whereas the canal goes south-west. Two streams that leave this stretch to our right are both the Kennet, one goes via Denford Mill and the other via Dun Mill. Some car parking can be found here on the corner of Dunmill Lock Bridge.

The footpath now crosses to the southern bank by means of the Dunmill Bridge. Take the path immediately to the right after crossing the bridge. Dunmill Lock is now on our left with Dun Mill itself on the northern bank. Fishing rights are now owned by Hungerford AA. Hungerford itself is on the horizon. A broad path leads to a stile just opposite the mill buildings.

The way proceeds for approximately three quarters of a mile with Hungerford clearly in view directly ahead. Over to the right (the northern side of the canal) is a thick hedge and beyond that a trout farm (best seen from the train).

When the canal was built in the late eighteenth century, there was no such thing as compulsory purchase, even if there was an Act of Parliament to give force to your venture. What this meant in practice was that as the canal progressed, every landowner had to be contacted and negotiated with before the land could be bought and the canal built. Sometimes the amount of work involved must have been extraordinary and this is amply demonstrated here. In this half-mile stretch before Hungerford, no fewer than twenty-eight different landowners had to be persuaded to sell their land at a price acceptable to both company and owner.

Central Hungerford is first reached by a small bridge next to a sanitary station (for navigators not walkers).

If in a hurry, the BR station can be found by turning left here (fifty yards). For preference, continue the walk to the next bridge and into town before turning back to the station via Park Street (the first left along the High Street).

Hungerford Town Bridge is reached within one hundred yards.

Turn right at the bridge (into Bridge Street) for the way to the A4 and two pubs (within 200 yards). Turn left for the High Street. Here there is a wide range of shops, cafes and pubs as well as the route previously mentioned back to the station. There is car parking at the station or in the middle of town. Early closing day is Thursday.

It is very difficult to enter Hungerford without thinking about the horrific events of 19th August 1987 when Michael Ryan run amuck and killed sixteen people including himself. How such a pleasant town can be struck down in such a way is difficult to imagine. How the people have been able to recover is even harder to imagine. Still to an extent they have and anyone who walks to Hungerford will share my appreciation for the place.

Hungerford does have a history and a character beyond Michael Ryan. Like a number of the places the K&A passes through, the town is an important stopping place. Here routes converge to cross the Kennet and a town at this spot was only natural. John of Gaunt became Lord of the Manor

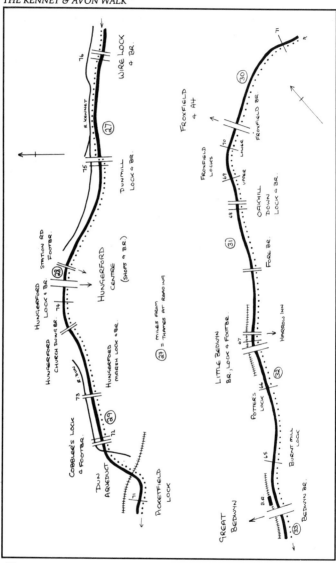

WIRE LOCK & BR.

76

R. KENNET

27

75

DUNMILL LOCK & BR.

STATION RD FOOTBR.

HUNGERFORD LOCK & BR. 74

28

HUNGERFORD CENTRE (SHOPS & BR.)

HUNGERFORD CHURCH SWING BR.

HUNGERFORD MARSH LOCK & BR.

73 & TUN

29

COBBLER'S LOCK & FOOTBR. 72

DUN AQUEDUCT

71

PICKETFIELD LOCK

27 = MILES FROM THAMES AT READING

FROXFIELD & A4

30

71

FROXFIELD BR.

70

LOWER

FROXFIELD LOCKS

69

UPPER

OAKHILL DOWN LOCK & BR.

68

FORE BR.

31

LITTLE BEDWYN BR., LOCK & FOOTBR.

67

HARROW INN

32

POTTER'S LOCK 66

65

BURNT MILL LOCK

B.R.

33

BEDWYN BR.

GREAT BEDWYN

in 1366 and it is said that any monarch passing through the town is given a Lancastrian red rose as token rent.

In the Civil War, the town housed both the roundhead Earl of Essex (before the first Battle of Newbury) and King Charles (before the second Battle of Newbury). The king stayed at the Bear Hotel on the A4 just north of the canal.

The Bear Hotel had another royal guest in December 1688. William of Orange had stopped in Hungerford (he stayed at Littlecote) during his triumphant march from Brixham to London. Messengers from King James arrived with a compromise and presented their case to William at the Bear Hotel. The prince's advisers urged him to reject the king's propositions and they continued their onward march via Windsor to London, where he was eventually crowned in 1689.

Trains back to Newbury are less romantic but more regular. Every hour and a half is a good approximation. There are no trains here on Sundays although British Rail runs three buses back to Newbury in the late afternoon/early evening. Normal buses are so few and far between, they're not worth mentioning.

4: THE K&A WALK
HUNGERFORD to PEWSEY

The route now takes us into rural Wiltshire where tranquil pastoral scenes become intertwined with industrial archaeology at the Bruce Tunnel and the celebrated Crofton Pumping Station. The canal has passed out of reach of the average London commuter and the M4 corridor, and so the bustle, noise and new housing estates are gradually being left behind. Villages seem more remote and less spoilt; the small towns retain their original shops rather than play host to the pre-packaged chains.

The canal itself has its ups and downs here. Its ups are reached just before the Bruce Tunnel where we reach the highest point on the navigation and water starts to flow down to the Avon. Its downs are the problems obtaining sufficient water to fill the pounds. The Crofton Flight was unnavigable when I walked the path because the water level was simply too low.

As far as Bedwyn trains are still available for transport to and fro. From Bedwyn things get tough and walkers have to resort to cunning if they want public transport to return them to their cars or hostels. The BR station at Pewsey looks tempting but doesn't often deliver and although Pewsey and Bedwyn are the closest of neighbours, no train ever joins the two. If pushed, a route back can be devised via Marlborough (enquire at the Marlborough Tourist Information).

Hungerford is the biggest town in this section and should be used for stocking up on provisions. Pewsey has a small number of shops, including a supermarket but is about three-quarters of a mile from the canal. There is a small supermarket at Great Bedwyn but little else en route. There are, as usual, pubs at various points all the way along.

A. HUNGERFORD to CROFTON

Distance:	6¹/₂ miles/11 kilometres
Map:	OS Landranger 174 (Newbury & Wantage)
Transport:	BR Reading (0734-595911)
	Un- (or partially) manned BR stations at Hungerford and (Great) Bedwyn
	There aren't many buses to speak of but some do visit Great

Bedwyn at peculiar times. Check with: Wiltshire & Dorset Bus Co. (0722-336858)

The National Express bus 602 that runs from Devizes via Marlborough (Lloyds Bank), Hungerford (Bear Inn) to Newbury in the morning may be of use (return trip in early evening). Phone 071-730-0202 for details.

Car Parks: Hungerford: Town centre and railway station
Little Bedwyn: Some on-road
Great Bedwyn: Some near railway station
Crofton: Near pumping station or by Crofton and/or Freewarren Bridges
Wilton: On-road

Tourist Info: Marlborough on 0672-513989

Walkers wishing to make this section into a round trip, or wishing to stop at a pub half way, have a choice. At Wilton (three-quarters of a mile south of the canal at Crofton) there is the Swan Inn. Alternatively you could stop at Great Bedwyn (after five miles) or go on to the Savernake Forest Hotel above the Bruce Tunnel (eight and a half miles). The sober alternative is simply to take a picnic and enjoy the interesting scenery at Crofton.

If you're joining the route from either the car park or the BR station at Hungerford, you should firstly make your way to the High Street where you turn right (after stocking up at the shops) and down left when you come to the town bridge. A prompt left turn at the canal will put you back onto the towpath.

Hungerford Wharf is on the other side of the canal and usually there are boats moored here. The stone building on the wharf was originally a storehouse. Within one hundred yards the path reaches Hungerford Lock.

The canal reached Hungerford in October 1798. A barge had navigated from Newbury loaded with a staircase made from dressed Portland stone (for Chilton Lodge) and a number of casks of Russian tallow (tallow is a type of fat used to make candles and soap).

There is an information notice at the lock and this describes how the wharf was originally developed as a gauging station where the carrying capacity of boats was officially assessed. The notice also bears a photograph of workers on the canal using an Archimedean screw pump. This highly primitive device can now be seen as an exhibit at the Crofton Pumping Station.

After the lock the canal bends slightly southwards and passes St. Lawrence's Church.

The church here was re-built in 1816 after the previous one had collapsed under the weight of a snowfall. The church is now constructed of much sturdier Bath stone which was shipped in using the newly constructed canal.

We pass a wooden swing bridge (the footpath right goes out to the A4 and hence onto Chilton Foliat and the Chilton Estate).

The walled garden at Chilton became a TV star in the late 1980s when the BBC used it to film its Victorian Kitchen Garden series.

The canal now bends back north. On the right the River Dun forms a marshy area and several small footbridges can be seen carrying paths across. This is Hungerford Marsh.

Hungerford Marsh is a BBONT (Berkshire, Buckinghamshire & Oxfordshire Naturalists' Trust) nature reserve. The excellent book that is provided free to every member of BBONT describes the reserve as 'unimproved rough grazing and reed bed, 11.2 hectares (twenty-eight acres) in area'. The book also says that 120 different bird species have been seen here over the last ten years. 120! It's enough to make you hang up your binoculars. I'd only seen about thirty-five along the entire K&A by this stage! Star of the show is apparently the snipe. Those who would like to join BBONT should write to 3 Church Cowley Road, Rose Hill, Oxford OX4 3JR. Selfish people will do it for the guide book alone.

We now pass over a stile and into an open field and up to Hungerford Marsh Lock.

Hungerford Marsh Lock is noteworthy for the fact that it has a swing bridge right in the middle of it. This was not due to the perverse nature of the builders but was forced upon them because the local authority refused the canal company permission to divert a public right of way. Modern councils should take note!

The area on the other side of the lock is called Freeman's Marsh. The rather splendid farm buildings are part of Hopgrass Farm. If you want to make the most of this right of way, it passes alongside the farm and up to the A4 where there is some room for parking in a lay-by.

Continue alongside the canal and through a gate up to Cobbler's Lock. A neat lock-keeper's cottage is on the northern side.

Just a few yards after the lock, and very easily missed, is the first aqueduct on the canal so far. Called the Dun Aqueduct, it has just three arches and allows the River Dun to pass from the northern side to the southern. You can see the river expanding liberally all over a field to the left. The aqueduct is actually much easier to spot from the train, so if you're coming back along the line keep an eye out for it.

After passing over a stile and alongside a chicken farm on the right, the route goes under a bridge and then the railway before bending sharply right. The next lock is Picketfield Lock. A further 300 yards brings us to Froxfield Bridge. Just before the bridge you can see a pig farm on the right (actually the nose finds it first!).

You are now in Wiltshire. Froxfield Bridge is on the border. Turn right here for the A4 and the Watermeadow Inn (quarter of a mile). Froxfield is worthy of attention for its imposing Somerset Hospital, an almshouse originally built in 1694 at the behest of the Duchess of Somerset to house 'thirty poor widows'.

The towpath now leads to three locks in quick succession (within half a mile of each other). The first is Froxfield Lower, then there's Froxfield Upper, followed by Oakhill Down. Fishing is now under the Nine Elms AA. The pound between upper and lower was very short of water as I passed. Mud and weed seemed to predominate. Restoration of Froxfield Upper Lock was supported by Marks & Spencer, no less. Presumably if the K&A Canal Trust don't like it, they can take it back.

Before Oakhill Down Lock, the path meets a minor road. Shortly after the lock, the road bends away left and we pass along an overgrown, narrow track with a willow plantation in a meadow to the northern side. The path passes under a small road bridge and the pleasant village of Little Bedwyn appears. Walk on to the railway footbridge.

Photographers will rush around here trying to decide which is the best angle in which to capture the lock, the railway, the canal, the village, the church (St. Michael's) etc. I don't think I succeeded necessarily.

The odd arrangement of bridges here reveals the history. The small footbridge over the canal was once a swing bridge. When the railway was built (1862) the company added the railway footbridge. This meant that the two halves of the village were cut off from one another. As a result, the new road bridge (just beyond the lock) was built. It all looks a bit higgledy-piggledy and not at all the sort of thing that an American visitor would understand.

Little Bedwyn is quite an ancient site. It once had a Roman camp and

Little Bedwyn

a Saxon mint. If you take the road on the left, opposite the footbridges, you will reach the Harrow Inn (150 yards). Great Bedwyn is about one and a quarter miles away.

The fishing rights now belong to the 'MDAA'. In order to stimulate your enthusiasm for the coming section, you have precisely one and a quarter miles to come up with some suggestions for the name. Manchester & Durham perhaps?

The path now passes under the road bridge and Great Bedwyn can be seen in the distance. Potter's Lock is quickly passed before the canal bends slightly right.

Chisbury Hill Fort is on the hill to the right (about three-quarters of a mile). Leading from there, Bedwyn Dyke earthworks crosses the canal just before the next lock. This dyke is one end of Wansdyke, a linear earthwork that runs from Inkpen (a hill south of Kintbury) right through to Bath and on to Bristol (although the western end is older and was built by other tribes). At some points the dyke is a significant feature and very deep. At others, like here, it's barely visible. An easily accessible good bit is at Morgan's Hill about five miles north of Devizes. One book I've read claims that the dyke was formed as a result of a giant who was stumbling around the area with a shovelful of soil. As he tripped, a load fell off and formed the

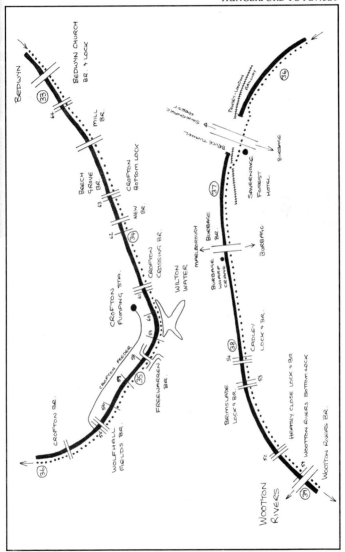

dyke. *Archaeologists, however, prefer the more rational explanation that it was built in the sixth century by the early Saxon king Caelwin. Apparently he was concerned about marauding Angles (from the Midlands) at the time and the dyke was built as a defensive barrier.*

The path now passes Burn Mill Lock (formerly the site of Burnt Mill) and then on to Great Bedwyn itself.

Walkers not stopping at Great Bedwyn should walk up to the road, bear left, turn right through some gates and back onto the towpath. A quicker route goes under the fence.

Those wishing to visit the village for interest, re-stocking or refreshment should turn right, pass over the railway bridge and continue up to the High Street. Those planning to return east should turn first right after the railway bridge and down to the unmanned BR station.

If you're planning to continue after Great Bedwyn, please remember that the trains that stop at Hungerford, Newbury and Reading terminate here and go no further. Obtaining public transport from here on will be difficult (if not impossible at convenient times). There is a small amount of car parking at the station.

The High Street has a small supermarket and two pubs (the Cross Keys and the Three Tuns). If you want some history, Great Bedwyn is home to the highly original stone museum (turn left when you get to the High Street). If you want a laugh, read the bus timetable at the bus stop just on the left here.

A sign on the village notice board informed me that Great Bedwyn was first in its heats of the Best Kept Village Competition. It's not that hard to see why. The judge's notes said 'lovely cricket ground', 'little litter' and 'no fly posting' - apart from their notice about the competition that is.

The town has a long history. But first the name. Although Bedwyn sounds as if it was originally a lost outpost of some rampaging Welsh prince, it isn't. Bedwyn, or 'bedwine', is the old Saxon name for bindweed. Boring, isn't it? However, things improve. Bedwyn was, for example, one of the famous, or infamous, 'rotten boroughs' (one in which there had been considerable depopulation but which still retained its original number of MPs. Such boroughs were inevitably corrupt). Bedwyn returned two MPs until the Reform Act of 1867.

The church (with its interestingly decorated tower) is Norman and contains the remains of Sir John Seymour. Sir John was father of Jane

Seymour, the third wife of Henry VIII (the one immediately after Ann Boleyn who produced Edward VI just before she died - remember?). It was Jane's brother, Edward, who assumed power as 'Protector of the Realm' when Henry died and her other brother, Thomas, who married Henry's widow, Catherine Parr. Both brothers were eventually executed (Thomas in 1549, Edward in 1552) for, basically, trying to usurp power.

Great Bedwyn had another famous son in the form of Thomas Willis, who was born here in 1621. He was one of the founder members of the Royal Society and conducted researches into diabetes and the circulation of blood around the body.

This section of the canal from Hungerford was opened on July 2nd 1799. The first barge carried fifty tons of coal and deals (sawn timber). Apparently this cargo was received with 'great demonstration of joy' and 'quantities' of beer were consumed at a 'great festivity'. No such rejoicing occurred with my arrival, so after a visit to the supermarket, I carried on to Crofton.

To continue on the path, retrace your steps until after you cross first the railway and then the canal at the bridges. Then pass through some metal gates to the right or take the under-the-fence short-cut. In both cases, the area on the other side of the fence is a boat yard. Pass to the right of a small hut and continue along the path.

Oh, before I forget, it's Marlborough & District. The fishing.

Our way rapidly leaves Great Bedwyn behind although we get a good view of St. Mary's Church for the first couple of hundred yards. Shortly we reach Church Bridge and Lock. The path now continues to a road bridge and out along a narrow, gravelly track. We now reach Beech Grove Bridge and Crofton Bottom Lock.

Crofton Bottom Lock is the first in a series (nine in about one and a half miles), called the Crofton Flight. These will take us to the summit of the canal. At this point some female pochard waylaid the author's attention for some minutes while he struggled with their identification.

After passing under an elegant high bridge with bushes growing on it, the path moves on to a lock with a cottage. Our way now goes through two stiles, on 200 yards and through two more stiles. The Crofton Pumping Station is now clearly in view on the right-hand side of the canal. The path passes up through a gate to a bridge, the Crofton Crossing Bridge, and, after a stile, to a lock.

Crofton Crossing Bridge bears the weight of a Roman road which proceeds north-west via Marlborough to Cirencester or south-east via Andover to Winchester and runs at almost exactly 90° to the canal. The southerly route is a relatively quick way to Wilton - should you need a quick way to Wilton. Walk down the track for about three quarters of a mile and turn right at the minor road. On the northern side there is an opportunity for car parking (if you brought your car with you that is).

Within one hundred yards, the next lock is reached near a signpost. Wilton Water is on the left and the pumping station is on the right. To visit the pumping station, cross the canal by means of the downstream gates of the lock. Turn left. A fence running up to the pumping station can now be seen about thirty yards away. Just after this, there is a path which runs off right through a tunnel under the railway to some steps. Pass up the right-hand steps to reach an explanatory notice and then the buildings. The entrance to the pump house (and the leat) can be found by passing to the right of the buildings.

Undoubtedly one of the key problems in the continuous running of the canal (or any canal) is maintaining the water level - particularly at the highest ends. Remember that these are artificial waterways that have no natural feed water. Every time a lock is used, water is lost downstream which isn't necessarily being replaced upstream. This is particularly the case with a short summit level where the water catchment is relatively small. Such is the problem on the K&A and such was the rationale for the Crofton Pumping Station.

The natural lake of Wilton Water, 300 yards south of the pumping house was used as a reservoir (after damming a small river to make it larger). Water was raised forty feet into the summit pound by the action of two steam beam engines; the first is an 1812 Boulton & Watt engine and the second was built in 1846 by Harvey's of Hayles in Cornwall. The Boulton & Watt is the oldest working beam engine in the world that is still in its original place doing its original job. Each engine pumps about eleven to twelve tons of water/minute (I make this 2,640 gallons) into a small channel called a leat, which wends its way for about a mile westwards to release its water into the canal just above Crofton Top Lock. When fully operational, two boilers were used with a third kept as a reserve.

The Earl of Ailesbury, who lived in the nearby mansion at Tottenham Park (about a mile and a quarter north-west) placed objections to the construction of the pumping house. Eventually go-ahead was given with

Crofton Pumping Station

the stipulation that the steam engines were to be made to consume their own smoke and that any engineman who caused any smoke would be sacked.

By 1958 the engines became unusable as the chimney had to be lowered for safety reasons. A diesel pump was installed, followed by an electric pump. The K&A Canal Trust bought the pumping station in 1967 and many hours of dedicated re-building of the Boulton & Watt engine culminated in the re-opening of the pumping house (by Sir John Betjeman) in April 1970. The 1846 engine went into steam again in November 1971.

The pumping house is open on most summer weekends and the pumps *can be seen. On certain weekends throughout the summer months, the engines are in steam. To find out which weekends, you should telephone the Trust's Devizes headquarters (0380-721279) or keep an eye open for posters at some locks.*

You should return to the canal and turn left and then right if you wish to visit the village of Wilton along with its pub, the Swan Inn. Wilton windmill is about another half a mile farther on from there. Turn right at the canal to continue the K&A walk.

B. CROFTON to PEWSEY

Distance:	7½ miles/12 kilometres
Map:	OS Landranger 174 (Newbury & Wantage) & 173 (Swindon, Devizes & surrounding area)
Transport:	BR Pewsey. NB: Trains are few and far between. Buses at Pewsey: Wiltshire & Dorset Bus Co. (0722-336858). W&D also pass through Wootton Rivers as do Kennet Coaches (0672-62715). The best route back to Hungerford is via Marlborough. See notes on the National Express bus 602 in section A. NB: Buses are not very frequent. There is no public transport from Pewsey back to Crofton.
Car Parks:	Crofton: Near pumping station or by Crofton and/or Freewarren Bridges Wilton: On-road Savernake Forest Hotel: On-road Burbage Wharf: On-road Wootton Rivers: Spaces near canal and in village near village 'centre' Pewsey: Large car park at wharf
Tourist Info:	Marlborough on 0672-513989

It must be emphasised that there is no public transport return for this half section.

The walk starts at the Wilton signpost opposite the Crofton Pumping Station. Turn left and pass the lock.

This is lock 60. A notice here says that the Crofton Flight was re-opened by two MPs in October 1988. Well, I'm afraid that the spirit might have been willing but the water ran short. The navigation between lock 60 and lock 59 was suffering from a severe fall in the pound. In fact, the whole flight was closed to navigation through lack of water, a victim of two long dry summers. The Canal Trust and British Waterways Board plan to try to overcome this problem with the installation of extra pumping power at Crofton. Until this happens the flight here may remain tricky.

Another lock is passed and the canal bends right. The path goes up to Freewarren Bridge and then down to the next lock.

The lock here, formerly known to its friends as 58, is now called Sam Farmer's Lock. The funds for its restoration were donated by the Samuel Farmer Trust. Sam, it appears, was an agriculturalist (ie. a farmer) and a philanthropist and lived at Little Bedwyn Manor. He died in 1926. So, if you fancy having a lock named after you, clearly you should give the British Waterways Board a call. By the way, there is an opportunity for some off-road parking just here.

After about 150 yards, the towpath passes the remains of a railway bridge, then locks 57 and 56. Here tall stands of poplar trees look tired after a long summer's photosynthesising. The broad, dirt path now leads up to Crofton Top Lock and, shortly thereafter, two derelict railway bridges.

Crofton Top Lock is the highest on the Thames side of the K&A canal summit (ie. it is the head of the eastern descent). You have come up fifty-two locks (and nearly 330 feet) in the thirty-five and a half miles/fifty-seven kilometres since leaving the Thames at Reading. We are now 450 feet higher than the tidal Thames. As you pass the lock, don't forget to look across to see the entry of the leat from the Crofton Pumping Station. If you want a peek at the Wilton windmill, cross to the top of the bridge and look back and over to the horizon.

The railway bridges along here used to carry the Midland and South-Western Junction Railway (originally called the Swindon, Marlborough and Andover Railway). This was an independent line that went to Swindon, Marlborough and Andover (bet you didn't guess), and joined with the Midland Railway at Cheltenham. It opened in July 1881. It went the way of all good lines in September 1961.

The path now continues up to and under a minor road bridge.

The path leading from the bridge to the left goes to the site of Wolf Hall. This was formerly the home of the Seymours and is where Henry VIII courted Lady Jane. Apparently Henry and his entourage took over the hall completely and the Seymours had to move out to live in the barn. Some in-laws are like that. The hall isn't very visible from the road and a detour isn't recommended.

Bruce Tunnel

The towpath is now a dirt track and is overshadowed by some massive and luxuriant oak, beech and ash trees. Almost unnoticed the canal enters into a deep cutting. After about three-quarters of a mile, we reach the Bruce (Savernake) Tunnel. Take the path that runs up the hill on the left about twenty to thirty yards before the tunnel itself.

This section is so different to anything we've met so far that it's worth dawdling a while. The cutting and the overhanging trees give you a feeling of being enclosed in a great, dank chasm. And then you meet the tunnel at the end which, for a moment, just a moment, you think may suddenly give birth to a huge, fire-breathing dragon. Of course, these feelings only occur after lunch.

The summit level of the K&A is just two miles long and the summit pound was one of the shortest in the country when first built. The tunnel is 502 yards long and quite wide and tall for a canal tunnel. There is no towpath, however. Instead, chains were fixed to the wall and bargemen used to haul themselves through. The horse, meanwhile, had a gentle stroll over the top.

The entrance of the tunnel mouth is a great brick archway and, all in all, a bit plain to look at. Above the eerie, gaping mouth is the only feature; a large stone plaque dedicating the tunnel to Thomas Bruce, Earl of Ailesbury. It expresses thanks for the 'uniform and effectual support' that he gave to the building of the K&A.

Over two million bricks were needed to build the tunnel. Most of these were made at the company's own brickworks next to the Caen Hill Locks at Devizes. I'll point them out when we get there.

The path that goes up to the Savernake forest comes as a shock. It's easily the steepest part of the east to west K&A Walk (those who have come all the way from London will have climbed the steeper Winter Hill) and reminded me just how flat this walk is. Don't worry, it doesn't last long.

The clear path runs through some woodland and larch plantings. After 200 yards we reach a driveway (left is the entrance to 'Ladywells'). Keep straight on, passing a house to your right. Within a few yards, the path crosses a minor road (Stibb Green to A4). Here on the left is the Savernake Forest Hotel.

The hotel is two star and open for coffee, tea and drinks on a non-resident basis.

Strictly speaking this isn't the Savernake forest. The forest proper lies to the north, has an area of about 4,000 acres and a circumference of about sixteen miles. Like the New Forest, it is a royal hunting forest and has been since the Norman conquest. The area is let at a peppercorn rent to Lord Ailesbury but, also like the New Forest, the general public is allowed access and there are numerous excellent walks.

There is a towpath sign on the road. This points walkers down a narrow but clear track alongside the hotel buildings. After a hundred yards or so a railway cutting appears on the right. Shortly thereafter the path goes down some steps, under the railway and, as if by magic, out to the canal which has reappeared from its underground excursion.

The chasm this side is not too dissimilar to that on the other. This could be a place of terrifying solitude if it wasn't for the railway just the other side of the bushes and the multitude of fishermen whose gear needs stepping over at roughly ten-yard intervals. There was a competition on and, as far as I could see, it was a pretty close tussle for the lead with nobody catching anything.

The canal emerges eventually from the cutting and passes under a tall bridge (Burbage Bridge) which carries the very busy A346

Andover-Marlborough road. Shortly after the bridge, on the northern bank, is the Burbage Wharf and Crane.

The splendid Burbage Bridge, designed by John Rennie, is an early example of a skew bridge - ie. one that isn't at right angles to the canal. When Rennie designed the bridge the techniques involved were only in their infancy and bridges before this were always built at 90° to the thing they were crossing. John Rennie, it may be remembered, was one of the country's premier bridge builders. It was Rennie's London Bridge that was dismantled and shipped to America in the 1970s.

Burbage Wharf was the nearest point to Marlborough, which never did get a direct canal link. The massive wooden crane is, disappointingly, a replica erected in the 1970s. The former one had to be removed.

The next stretch of path is grassy, overgrown and uneven. You will get wet legs here after dew or rain. After what seems like eternity but is, in fact, only three-quarters of a mile, we reach Cadley Lock next to a tiny cottage and a bridge.

You can now proudly say that you are 'over the hill'. The canal water from now on will end up in the Avon and not in the Thames. Cadley Lock is the highest lock at the head of the western descent. Observant walkers will immediately notice that the lock gates now face in the opposite direction. Just forty-seven locks and thirty-eight miles/sixty-one kilometres to the Avon at Bath and fifty-six miles/ninety kilometres to the end of the walk at the floating harbour in Bristol.

Within 150 yards of easy walking, the second downhill lock is met. The path passes over the bridge (through two gates) and back down to the canal.

Brimslade Lock and Bridge dissect the Brimslade farm neatly in two. A notice warns walkers to keep to the path here and not to wander over the private property to left and right. The fine-looking farm house festooned with chimneys on the southern side is reputed to date back to the sixteenth century.

The towpath now passes along a mown grass track and passes Heathy Close Lock with its attendant bridge. Within a couple of hundred yards the path reaches Wootton Rivers with its lock and bridge. There is a small lock-keeper's hut on the left.

Wootton Rivers lock will be the last we shall see for a while as the canal now enters the fifteen-mile pound. The next lock is at Devizes. The relatively flat land between Wootton Rivers and Devizes is called the Vale

Dredger near Wootton Rivers

of Pewsey, an area of low greensand and clay surrounded by chalky downs. Here the land drains into the Hampshire Avon. Don't confuse this river with the one we'll meet later. This Avon winds its way through Salisbury and the New Forest before flowing into the sea at Christchurch.

Wootton Rivers is a delightful village and well worth a visit. Turn right at the bridge, cross the canal and walk on for about half a mile. Virtually all the houses here are thatched, even the local pub, the Royal Oak (400 yards from the canal on the right). The church, St. Andrew's, has achieved fame for being short of funds. When some restoration was needed just before the First World War, the money ran out and the church clock *could not be restored to its former glory. Instead, one Jack Spratt (believe it or not) rebuilt the timepiece out of bits of farm machinery, bedsteads, bicycles and so on. His handiwork can also be seen on the face of one of the clocks where letters spelling out GLORY BE TO GOD have replaced the more conventional numbers (when I was there it was Y past G). A similar clock can be seen on another village building further along the street.*

The village is well stocked with car parking spaces both near the canal (there are spots marked at an angle to the road) and farther into the village near the community centre. There is, sadly, no village shop - if there was one the village really would be complete. Near the canal bridge there is a bus stop but little promise of a bus. Should you maintain hope, the telephone numbers of the relevant companies are provided at the head of this section.

Leave Wootton Rivers on the towpath on the south side of the canal. Within a hundred yards the broad grassy track passes Wootton Rivers Farm Bridge to our right. Beyond is Martinsell Hill, the site of a hill fort. A second bridge, Current (or Carrel) Bridge, is passed within 300 yards.

This section is rich in weeping willows and other ornamental trees. The river was being dredged here as I passed. The British Waterways Board has a floating dredger that was scouring out the silt and decayed weed and dumping it, thankfully, on the opposite (northern) bank.

Despite this flurry of activity, this stretch had a spectacular display of red admiral butterflies. Like many butterflies, the red admiral is strongly territorial and spends much of its day patrolling its ground and repelling rivals. Unlike many butterflies, however, (but like the painted lady), the admiral (or 'admirable' as it was known in the eighteenth century) is a one-way migrant. No red admiral over-winters in this country; they all die out. We are totally dependent on spring-summer imports for our admirals and ladies. Apart from the extraordinary concept of such a delicate creature travelling such enormous distances, it seems odd that the insects should migrate and breed in this country without leaving offspring for the following season. This peculiar evolutionary deadend would appear to go against all the basic premises of survival and evolution. Is it a practice left over from a time when they were either able to survive and/or return to their homelands? Or are these the scouts testing the land and awaiting the time when they will be able to survive here? Whatever, I suppose we should be grateful that they do come and that we can still enjoy the beauty of these ill-fated individuals.

Martinsell Hill used to be the site of an ancient ritual. On Palm Sunday local villagers walked to the top of the hill (and back again presumably). Why they did this is unclear although some people believe that mystical ground forces pulled them to the site. Similar rituals were held at Silbury Hill (near Avebury) and Cley Hill (near Warminster). As it wasn't Palm Sunday, the magnetic force wasn't up to much and I continued along the canal.

The towpath passes under a minor road bridge at New Mill. (OS Maps indicating a PH here are wrong). The scenery is now quite hilly and the canal is on the side of an incline; the land left drops down to a minor road, the land right goes up to Martinsell Hill. The path passes a new(ish) one storey building on our right and goes under a bridge.

This quiet section (my notes say that my footsteps were the noisiest thing about) is only spcradically interrupted by the belligerent farting of the Inter-City 125s as they plough their way to the south-west. The line is now farther away than at any stage of the walk so far and will get further. Once past Pewsey it disappears from reach for good and we have to wait until Bradford-on-Avon for any further assistance from BR.

We pass under a farm bridge which has a stile off left. This is Pains Bridge. If you wish to go to Pewsey and want to avoid walking along a main road, take this left turn. Continue straight (it turns into a minor road after passing under the railway) and continue until you reach the Pewsey-Burbage main road. Turn right and the centre of town is about quarter of a mile.

With Pewsey now in view over to the left, the canal bends gently right and meets a main road (A345 Pewsey-Marlborough) at Pewsey Wharf.

Pewsey Wharf has a K&A Canal Trust building which houses toilets and possibly - it was shut when I tried the door - somewhere for a cup of tea. There is a large car park here. Across the canal is the French Horn public house.

Those wanting to get to Marlborough (for the A4 or M4) should turn right at this bridge. Marlborough is about five miles north.

For Pewsey turn left. There is no footpath along this busy main road for about half a mile. Keep to the road for the BR station (very few trains stop here) and the town centre (about 300 yards beyond the station). Pewsey isn't a tourist resort but it has a small number of shops and some pubs. *Early closing is Wednesday. Few buses go through Pewsey and none take you back to Hungerford or Bedwyn. Enquiries should be made at the phone numbers quoted for other destinations.*

5: THE K&A WALK
PEWSEY to DEVIZES

We are now firmly within the heart of ancient Wiltshire and this section of the walk is entirely within the Vale of Pewsey, a part of the North Wessex Downs Area of Outstanding Natural Beauty. To both the north and south of the canal run ribbons of chalk downland. On this herb-rich turf, man has lived for thousands of years and some of his most celebrated constructions are found here: to the north, Avebury stone circle, Silbury Hill and the West Kennet long barrow; to the south, Stonehenge.

The canal along this stretch meanders around the contours and manages a full fifteen miles without a single lock. As a consequence the canal blends even farther into the scenery and becomes even less like an industrial waterway than hitherto. This is peaceful and relaxing walking territory. With the dismissal of the Inter-City line at Pewsey, the pace now slows to a gentle stroll. Nowhere along the entire route are we as remote as we are along this section. This is as wild as central, southern England gets. This may come as a shock to northerners, who might still find a trace of bustle hidden somewhere in the crevices but it'll be a blessed relief to those who have come west from London or east from Bath and Bristol.

Such remoteness doesn't help the walker from a transport point of view. But fear not. Things at Devizes are much better than they are at Pewsey. Well, a bit, anyway. Buses go north and south with some regularity, even if they don't necessarily go east or west with any frequency worth discussing. There is the blessing of a school bus that leaves Devizes and goes to Pewsey at about ten minutes to four on school days only. Otherwise, it's the circular walk, the B&B, the thumb or a link via Marlborough. This latter return trip can be achieved by taking a bus from Devizes to Avebury then Marlborough (No. 49) and then another one (No. 6) from Marlborough to Pewsey. There's also the National Express.

Devizes is the biggest town in this section and can be relied on for stocking up with provisions (early closing is Wednesday). Pewsey has a small number of shops, including a supermarket but is about three-quarters of a mile from the canal. As before, there are plenty of pubs at various points all along the way.

A. PEWSEY to ALL CANNINGS

Distance:	6 miles/10 kilometres
Map:	OS Landranger 173 (Swindon, Devizes & surrounding area)
Transport:	BR Pewsey (no trains along course of canal west) Wiltshire & Dorset Bus Co.'s No.12 runs from Devizes to Pewsey on school days ONLY. To check ring: 0722-336858. For information on buses ring Marlborough tourist information office or Thamesdown Buses (0793-523700). There are no buses running from All Cannings to Pewsey. The National Express coach 602 runs from Trowbridge via Devizes to Marlborough (and on to Hungerford, Newbury and London) in the morning and returns in the early evening. Check on 071-730-0202.
Car Parks:	Pewsey: At wharf Honey St. & Stanton St. Bernard: Limited on-road All Cannings: On-road
Tourist Info:	Marlborough on 0672-513989

If you're joining the route from the BR station at Pewsey or from the centre of town, you should firstly make your way to the wharf by turning left and walking along the main A345 Marlborough road until you reach the canal. This is about three-quarters of a mile, half a mile of which is on a main road without a pavement. If you pass the French Horn, you've gone too far. Enter the car park (on the right) and turn left at the canal to pass under Pewsey Bridge and on to Devizes.

The first section of path is a dirt track. On the opposite bank boats are moored. In just under half a mile, we reach Bristow Bridge - a splendid brick arch structure that carries the minor road from Wilcot to Marlborough. Here we walk up to the road, cross the canal and descend to the other bank where the towpath proceeds through Stowell Park. Our way runs through a leafy cutting and past two pill boxes. The scenery opens out on the right to form parkland. The canal is soon crossed by Stowell Park Suspension Bridge.

The path here is surrounded by luxuriant woodland: tall ash trees and thick hazel scrub. The fine house about half a mile over to the north is Stowell Park. The dilapidated looking footbridge that passes over the top of us is constructed from jointed iron bars and is apparently the only

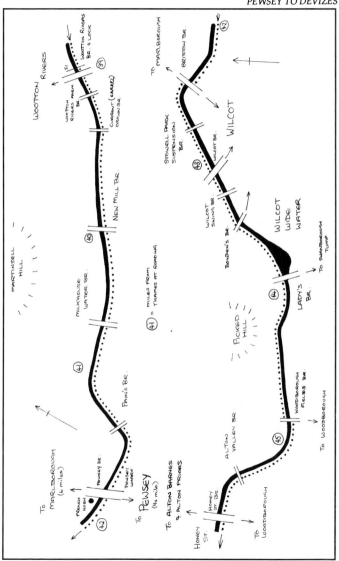

WOOTTON RIVERS

WOOTTON RIVERS BR. & LOCK

51

39

WOOTTON RIVERS BR.

CURRENT (BARGE) BR.

NEW MILL BR.

40

MILKHOUSE WATER BR.

MARTINSELL HILL

41 = MILES FROM THAMES AT READING

41

PAIN'S BR.

TO MARLBOROUGH (6 miles)

FRENCH HORN

PEWSEY BR.

PEWSEY WHARF

PEWSEY

42

TO MARLBOROUGH

TO PEWSEY (1/4 mile)

TO ALTON BARNES & ALTON PRIORS

HONEY ST. BR.

HONEY ST.

TO WOODBOROUGH

ALTON VALLEY BR.

TO WOODBOROUGH

45

WOODBOROUGH FIELDS BR.

TO WOODBOROUGH

PICKED HILL

LADY'S BR.

44

TO SWANBOROUGH TUMP

WILCOT WIDE WATER

BENSON'S BR.

WILCOT SWING BR.

WILCOT BR.

43

WILCOT

STOWELL PARK (SUSPENSION) BR.

TO MARLBOROUGH

BRISTOW BR.

42

101

surviving one of its type.

The canal at this point and for some miles on was, at the time of my visit, thick with duckweed. Each tiny, flat, round leaf is an individual plant (properly called a thallus). It spreads by producing buds which break off to form a new plant - hence its ability to cover an area of water like this so quickly. The plant does flower but rarely, and then with only a very small structure hidden on the margin of the leaf. There are actually four different types in this country but it was cold and I'd only just got over chicken pox and everything...so it's up to you to identify the species exactly. I satisfied myself by encouraging a group of slothful looking mallards to get on with some biological weed control.

After a thatched cottage to our right, a metalled road arrives to accompany us to the next bridge. We stay on the towpath, separated from the road by a hawthorn hedge. A small village with more thatched houses can be seen on the left (south). The towpath now goes under Wilcot Bridge and on to Wilcot Swing Bridge.

Turn left at Wilcot Bridge for Wilcot, a small, pleasant village with a pub, the Golden Swan (300 yards). The pub also has some B&B accommodation. Some of the houses in Wilcot were built (in the early nineteenth century) when the village of East Stowell was enclosed, the locals thrown out and their village turned into Stowell Park.

The church (Holy Cross - burnt down and rebuilt in 1876) is visible from the canal at Wilcot Swing Bridge.

The prominent hill that now appears in front of us is Picked Hill. The lump on it is not a cow or some really interesting folly but a triangulation pillar.

It is at this point, between Wilcot Bridge and Wilcot Swing Bridge, that the proposed Bristol & Salisbury Canal would have joined the K&A. The route to Salisbury (via Old Sarum, Amesbury and Upavon) would then have given a link to Southampton via the proposed Salisbury & Southampton Canal. There was a rush of support for the idea in 1792 but enthusiasm was quickly diluted by all the other building projects and, by 1797, it was virtually forgotten and was never revived.

About 200 yards after Wilcot Swing Bridge is Bowdens Bridge (another opportunity to turn left and go into Wilcot should craving for Wadworth's brews get too strong). The canal now broadens to form an ornamental lake in the grounds of Wilcot Manor. Lady's Bridge, covered with ivy and bramble, can be seen in the near distance.

As at Benham Broad, just after Newbury, Lady Wroughton would only let the canal company cross her land if they agreed to the construction of this area of 'wide water' together with the ornamental Lady's Bridge. They agreed (I suppose they had to) and the work was done in 1808. The bridge is very nice, if a little over the top for a farm bridge. Dare one have a greater regard for the little, rustic, brick bridges that we've gotten used to? Whatever you might feel about it, it still feels deliciously rude to sneak underneath the canopy of its broad archway. What would Lady Wroughton have thought of we plebs taking such liberties with her arches? Botanists may also find the western side interesting as the plants (such as hartstongue fern) cling to the lady's intimate little nooks and crannies without shame.

If you take the ultimate challenge and climb up and cross the bridge, you will be able to take a farm track down to a minor road. Here, just on the other side of the road, is Swanborough Tump. Not much to look at but believed to be the site where Alfred the Great wrote his will when under attack by the Danes.

The broad grass path continues along the northern bank with a barbed wire fence, a massive field and Picked Hill on the right. Notices tell us that the fishing rights have changed from Pewsey & District A A to Devizes AA.

Picked Hill is the first chance we get to see some ancient Wiltshire field terraces or strip lynchets (we get another chance near Horton). Lynchets are those ridges of earth which form on the sides of hills that have been ploughed. Basically, the disturbed soil creeps down the hill under gravity and accumulates in these small banks. Where the soil is not disturbed (by subsequent agriculture or earthworks), the mounds can last for many hundreds of years and are held fast by the close-knit turf. They are a good tell-tale sign of a Celtic field system. The field terracing at Picked Hill is thought to be a relic of mediaeval farming and is just one of the many indications of the activity of man in these apparently bare hills.

Indeed, the downland to the north of the canal at this point is littered with hill forts, neolithic camps, long barrows, tumuli and ancient roadways. There's a deserted village (Shaw village), a stone circle (Avebury), various enclosures and defensive workings (such as Wansdyke). This area must have been a good land for primitive farmers and, presumably, reasonable to defend against marauding hordes of all descriptions.

The hill across the field that sports a tuft of pine trees is Woodborough

Hill.

The towpath returns to the southern bank at the next bridge: Woodborough Fields Bridge. Turn left here for Woodborough village (three-quarters to one mile).

The three large concrete blocks that you see here at the northern end of the bridge, together with others you may have seen and will see, were all part of the anti-tank defences of the Second World War.

If you stand on Woodborough Fields Bridge and look north-west, you will see one of the Wiltshire white horses. Why the people of eighteenth and nineteenth century Wiltshire had this craze for carving horses on the hills is unclear but they make a pleasant diversion. This one, Alton Barnes, was made in 1812 and is about one and a quarter miles north of the canal on a hill called Milk Hill. It was paid for by Robert Pile of Manor Farm, Alton Barnes. Seemingly, one John Thorpe, an itinerant painter, designed it (whilst standing on Honey Street Bridge) and was given £20 to build it by Mr Pile. Thorpe left the design but disappeared with the £20. A local man ended up cutting the turf and finishing the job. Thorpe was later hanged although whether it was related to this matter or not isn't clear. The horse is square at 166' high and 160' wide. It looks in proportion because of the angle of the hill. As part of the country's attempts to eradicate landmarks, the horse was grassed over during the war and uncovered again in 1945.

Pass over a stile (or limbo under the cross-bar) to return to the canal towpath which is now a pleasant grassy track. The canal bends north as it follows the contours. The village to our left is Woodborough. Shortly after the canal turns, the towpath passes the remnants of a bridge (bricked area on either side of canal). There is a public footpath that runs off left from here in the general (but not specific) direction of Woodborough. We continue under Alton Valley Bridge.

Just after Alton Valley Bridge the canal passes over one tributary of the Hampshire Avon. From here the river joins other tributaries to flow through Salisbury and thence to the sea at Christchurch. This is the first River Avon to be met on the K&A walk, we meet the other one that goes to Bristol just after we pass the outskirts of Trowbridge. There are, in fact, four River Avons in England. The other two are: the Stratford Avon (Shakespeare's one) that runs into the River Severn, and a lesser known one that rises in Dartmoor and goes to the sea at Salcombe.

The view of the white horse improves as we progress along the path. Just to the right of the horse - and not visible from here - is an archaeological site called Adam's Grave. This area of the hill is called Walker's Hill. Once upon a time, so a local story goes, a young lady was strolling across the hill on a warm summer's day. As she approached the barrow of Adam's Grave, she heard an army of horses progressing across the hill. As she passed the barrow, the noise suddenly stopped. I strained hard but could only hear a farm tractor in the far distance - I think it was a real one.

In about quarter of a mile, the towpath reaches Honey Street Bridge. To continue the walk, pass under the bridge. If you wish to visit Honey Street itself or Alton Barnes, go up to the road and turn right.

Honey Street is a tiny village set on the banks of the canal. The wharf here used to be the home of Robbins, Lane & Pinnegar, a boat building company that supplied many of the narrowboats and other vessels that plied the K&A. The boats were launched sideways into the canal. The sight before us (on the northern bank) suggests that such activity is long gone. The area is now mostly a repository for blue plastic containers and old oil drums.

A portion of the Ridgeway footpath passes through Honey Street. The main body of this most ancient of old roadways goes from Overton Hill near Avebury to Streatley on Thames but it has been extended both north and south. The northern end follows the Icknield Way up to Ivinghoe near Tring. The southern end is in the process of being taken (with the support of the Ramblers' Association) from Avebury right down to Lyme Regis (although there is another leg to the Bristol Channel). Unlike many long-distance footpaths (and like this one), the Ridgeway is a genuine route in that it was a thoroughfare way back into prehistory. Immigrant Neolithic (late Stone Age, 4000 BC) farmers from Brittany and Spain are said to have passed along it as they settled into Wiltshire, Berkshire and Oxfordshire. Goods and workers have been transported or have travelled along the green roadway ever since. Even today, it is constantly busy with short and long-distance ramblers making the most of the splendid walking turf and superb scenery. Come back and do it after the K&A walk.

Large parts of Alton Barnes (about 400 yards north in the direction of the horse) belong to New College, Oxford; the land having been endowed by a Bishop of Winchester. He got it because in 825 King Egbert had given it to the church of St Peter and St Paul in Winchester. I don't know, all these people who can give whole villages away as presents! Alton Barnes has the benefit of a small (Spar) shop, should provisions be running low.

The towpath continues after the bridge along the southern side of the canal. Within 300 yards we reach the Barge Inn.

The route along here is made mildly interesting by the terraced gardens (most notably the vegetable plot) that are attached to the houses that run close to the northern bank of the canal.

The Barge Inn originally had its own brewery, bakehouse and slaughterhouse and was able to supply passing canal boats with all their bodily needs (well, food-wise anyway). It still does, to some extent. The original building was burnt down in 1858 but was rebuilt within six months and quickly got back to business.

If you take advantage of the wooden seats outside the pub, your view north is now taken up almost entirely with chalk downland; an apparently stark landscape which is one of our most important wild flower habitats. It is one of those strange ironies that this man-made environment, produced by wholesale destruction of a former habitat, is now so treasured and protected. In prehistory this was forest. Man altered it by clearing the trees and then intensively grazing it. It is a habitat dominated by sheep and rabbits, close cropping of the grass allowing the survival of the ancient turf. There are plants here which can only survive if they are left undisturbed - species which are poorly adapted to rapid colonisation of new territory; bastard toadflax, field fleawort, chalk milkwort and others. The downs are also justly prized for their orchids; bee, frog, burnt, fragrant, green-winged and pyramidal.

Now this man-made environment is endangered by man himself in his ever-pressing desire for increased cereal production. Large tracts of downland have been ploughed and, effectively, lost to some wild flowers for ever. As a result English Nature, formerly the Nature Conservancy Council, has established a downland nature reserve (the Pewsey Downs National Nature Reserve) off the Honey Street to Marlborough Road near Mr Pile's white horse. This latter attraction, incidentally, should still be visible to the north.

The canal bends right and passes under Stanton Bridge. Turn right here to go to the small village of Stanton St. Bernard that nestles under Milk Hill.

I saw somewhere that Stanton has a shop but I was unable to find it (apologies if there is one). Everybody agrees, however, that there is definitely no pub.

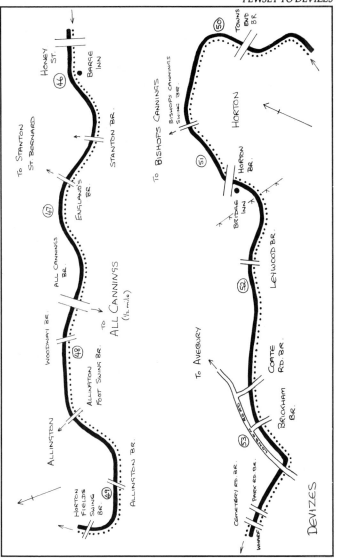

As you wander through this placid countryside and alongside what could be easily mistaken for one of nature's waterways, it's easy to forget that the canal was dug by the sweat of man. Although there are whole books on the lives and genius of the canal designers and ample discussion of their financial backers, not much gets said about the workmen who physically dug the canals. Part of the problem is that we are all to familiar with the bulldozer, the ten-ton truck, the ready-mix concrete lorry and the way that housing estates seem to appear overnight. The K&A was dug by men armed only with picks, shovels and wheelbarrows. They were occasionally assisted by horses and tramways but mostly it was hard, back-breaking graft and not the stuff of a good history book.

Life for the canal cutters, who were called navigators - later shortened to navvies, must have been awful. A large number of them were locals, pulled off the land for a month or two before returning to their farms when the work was done. But by the turn of the century, when this section of the K&A was built, the experienced navvy moved from one project to the next; living in rough camps. One estimate suggests that 50,000 men were so employed at the height of canal mania in the 1790s. Some were English peasants thrown off the land after the enclosure acts, some were from the Fens (experienced in digging drains), some were vagrants and some Scots and Irish. All must have been desperate.

Perhaps because of their circumstances, they were a pretty unruly lot and must have had a major impact on the small rural communities through which the canal passed. Farmers were said to live in fear for their crops, animals and, presumably, their wives and daughters. Things weren't helped by the canal companies. It wasn't so much that the rates of pay were low (the average in 1790 was twelve to eighteen old pennies per day) but that the companies often couldn't pay in ready cash. In 1797, when the banks refused the company advance funds because of uncertainty over the situation in the Napoleonic wars, the K&A navvies were paid in twenty-one day promissory notes. The navvies could normally only 'spend' these with particular tradesmen who usually insisted on discounting their value.

The one thing you can say for the job (if indeed there is anything to be said for it) is that they have left their own substantial and wonderful monument. How many of us can say that something we've done or contributed to will give pleasure to people some ten generations hence?

Further round, the canal begins to snake and weave along the valley. Our way passes under England's Bridge which proffers another opportunity to visit Stanton St. Bernard by turning right. The path now runs for about one mile, past a splendid stand of willow trees on the north bank, to All Cannings Bridge. Just before the bridge, there is a degated gate next to a towpath waymark post (points to Honey Street left and Devizes right). Turn off left here should you wish to visit All Cannings village.

The Kings Arms pub, 'Spar' shop and the toilets can be found after half to three-quarters of a mile by walking along the minor road and taking the second right turn. Turn left at the T-junction and these facilities will be found shortly thereafter.

All Cannings is a pleasant little village ('though recently expanded on the canal side) with a large village green overlooked by a mostly fifteenth century church (All Saints). Buses run to Devizes from here, but, alas, not to Pewsey.

All Cannings appears to lay claim to a story that I've seen repeated in SO many different guide books about SO many different villages that it MUST be true, mustn't it? Its ubiquitousness is mirrored in its generic title of the Wiltshire moonraker legend. Apparently, some local eighteenth century rogues smuggled some brandy kegs and hid them in the village pond. Some time later they were just in the process of recovering their bounty when the excisemen turned up (boo, hiss). Our cheeky but lovable villains claimed that they were raking for the cheese that they had seen in the pond. On investigation, the dastardly excisemen (boo, hiss) decided that this was merely the reflection of the full moon and that our heroes were nowt but simple country folk and obviously incapable of evil mischief. It's not even a very good story really but that's country lore for you.

B. ALL CANNINGS to DEVIZES

Distance: 6 miles/10 kilometres

Map: OS Landranger 173 (Swindon, Devizes & surrounding area)

Transport: Believe it or not buses run from Devizes to All Cannings - if spasmodically. Check with MC Travel on 0225-704528; Bodman Coaches 0380-722393 or Wilts & Dorset 0722-336855. If you are returning to Pewsey, there are two recommended routes. Wiltshire & Dorset's No.12 runs from Devizes to

Pewsey on school days ONLY. It leaves Devizes at 15.47. Alternatively take the Thamesdown No.49 to Marlborough (via Avebury) and then the Wilts & Dorset No.6 from Marlborough to Pewsey. See also the note on the National Express coach in part A.

Car Parks: All Cannings: On road
Devizes: At wharf (well signposted) or in town (never more than quarter of a mile distant)

Tourist Info: Devizes on 0380-729408

If you're joining the route from the centre of All Cannings, make your way north on the Allington/Stanton St. Bernard road. The canal will be reached at All Cannings Bridge within half a mile. Turn left to continue the walk to Devizes: a towpath signpost (on the Pewsey side of the bridge) points the way.

As you rejoin the path you might notice the bent metal rack that sits alongside the bridge on the towpath side of the canal. Indeed you may have seen similar racks full of long wooden beams on previous occasions. The planks held in the racks are called 'stop-planks' and are used by the waterway workers to board up a section of the canal to hold back the water in a kind of temporary dam when it has to be drained for repair.

The towpath is now a good, broad, grass track. Within a couple of hundred yards, we pass under Woodway Bridge. Turn left here if you've forgotten something in All Cannings. Continue on for another 300 yards to Allington Foot Swing Bridge.

The canal feels very exposed along this stretch and it must be pretty bleak in a northerly wind with snow in the air. All Saints Church, All Cannings is now visible to our left. If village bagging, you could take the footbridge right to Allington. Less enthusiastic walkers will be rendered even less enthusiastic with the news that the village has neither shop nor pub. For some reason, the duckweed gave out just here and the canal was clear of the stuff. But why?

If you turn right at Woodway Bridge and take the right-hand of three public rights of way over to Cannings Cross Farm, you can then take a footpath up, past Rybury Camp to Tan Hill. It's about one and a half miles altogether with a climb of about 525 feet (160 metres). Tan Hill is the highest point in the whole of Wiltshire at 964 feet (294 metres). It's said that ghosts have been seen on Tan Hill in the shape of a phantom cortège. Some shepherds once saw a horse-drawn wagon laden with a coffin, followed by a group of men. On top of the coffin was a gold crown. Just as the wagon drew level with the shepherds - it vanished into thin air! Was it an apparition of a former Celtic burial scene or the result of a Wadworth's carry out? We'll never know.

What we do know is that the area of All Cannings Cross is quite important archaeologically for there is evidence that an early Iron Age village of the Hallstatt period was once built here. The Hallstatts were the first Celtic people, the name coming from a village in Austria where they extracted salt. Indeed, salt, iron and efficient early farming techniques were the basis of their wealth and success, and the Halstatts spread firstly across Europe and then into Britain in about the seventh century BC, bringing their skills with them. Here, at All Cannings Cross, the village consisted of round thatched huts and there is evidence of iron smelting and of some seventy-five pits where corn, peas and beans were stored. A large urn and several swan's-neck pins have also been found. The furnace used for iron smelting is thought to be quite advanced with a special outlet at the bottom so that slag could be easily removed. An interesting feature of the many finds here were the human skull fragments. Many were cut, perforated and polished, as if they had been used as ornaments or religious relics of some kind.

We now pass another defunct swing bridge (brick work but no bridge) and then, about three-quarters of a mile after the Allington Footbridge, we reach Allington Bridge. Extensive dredging is evidenced here on the footpath side. The canal, instead of taking a direct course across the flat plain before us, now deviates north into a lumpy semi-circle.

The canal bends abruptly right (by Horton Fields Swing Bridge) and then left. On the right bank there is a fine stand of mature willow trees. Our view to the left is blocked by a high hawthorn hedge. We pass a small cottage on the right-hand bank. The canal then almost immediately bends right to pass under a minor road at Townsend Bridge.

Turn left here for Horton (no pubs or shops) or a sneaky short cut to the Bridge Inn on the other side of the semi-circle. It could save a third of a mile! Honest folk will, of course, continue and will be rewarded with the knowledge that at a point just before the canal bends sharply left (again) they notch up their 50th mile since the Thames. Alternatively you could turn right at the bridge for Allington. Although why would be a good question.

Large portions of Horton and the surrounding country are part of the Crown Estate (in fact over 9,500 acres). Both Horton and Bourton (to the north) are small agricultural villages with ancient farms and some timber-framed buildings.

This part of the path was thick with black slugs (actually the grey field slug - Milax - recognised as being uniformly grey all over with no fringe or under colour) which had presumably come off the corn fields looking for something to eat. Grey field slugs are one of the two most important pest slugs for the farmer. They are particularly partial to potatoes but will also happily chew on cereal crops. One of the important consequences of stopping stubble burning is, or will be, the increase in slug numbers. Burning off the stubble was a great surface steriliser and it is highly likely that slugs (and a number of other pests and diseases) will become more important as a pest as a result of its cessation. The main problem to walkers, however, is to avoid stepping on the pesky varmints.

The canal now bends sharp left to point us due west. We have reached the zenith of our semi-circle and there follows a straight section of about half a mile.

The hills in front of us are part of Roundway Down. Here in July 1643, the Royalists had one of their good days when they routed a weary Roundhead army. Farther right, with two TV masts and a clump of trees atop it, is Morgan's Hill. Both hills are swathed in ancient sites. On Roundway Hill is Oliver's Castle (a hill fort), several tumuli and a long barrow. Morgan's Hill has tumuli, an enclosure, and various barrows as well as the defensive earthwork known as Wansdyke. Farther down the hillsides, you may also be able to pick out the traffic passing along the A361 Devizes - Avebury road.

It was roughly at this point that I passed a woman with a dog. It suddenly occurred to me that this was the first person (and the first dog) that I'd seen since leaving Pewsey Wharf about eight and a half miles back. To my additional surprise, three more people followed on within a minute. I was to see nobody else until I was nearly into Devizes, which, by the way, is now just over three miles away.

If you pass some neat piles of what appear to be grass cuttings along the side of the canal, they are, in fact, heaps of duckweed that have been dragged out of the water.

A further mile takes the canal past a pill box and left to point south-west and on towards Devizes. Shortly (100 yards) we pass Bishops Cannings Swing Bridge.

Turn right here (and bear left) for Bishops Cannings and The Crown public house (about half a mile). The pub is actually part of the Crown Estates mentioned earlier. If you think that Saint Mary's Church bears a passing resemblance to Salisbury Cathedral take a gold star. The bishops of Salisbury owned the estate from Domesday times right up to 1858 (when it was sold to the Crown) and this no doubt influenced the style. The oldest bits of the church date from around 1150. At least it's more of a Salisbury-mimic than the church at Theale.

Incidentally, the Thamesdown bus No.49 passes through Bishop's Canning on its way to Devizes or Avebury/Swindon/Marlborough should you wish to duck out early.

After a further half mile, the path reaches Horton Bridge. Here the Bridge Inn stares down at the canal towpath like a troll, daring us to pass without visiting it.

If you turn left on the road here, you pass back through Horton and on to Townsend Bridge (remember that?). Turn right for a quick route to the A361. A road also carries straight on to the village of Coate.

If not visiting the pub, pass under the bridge and alongside some moored boats on the right-hand bank. Within a short distance the scenery and sense of hearing is dominated by some high, buzzing power cables.

The canal again bends right and reaches Leywood Bridge.

The large institutional - looking buildings that are now appearing to the left of a small copse on our right are the Victorian barrack buildings belonging to the Wiltshire Regiment. Beyond the barracks is the village of Roundway and, after that, Roundway Hill and Down. The barracks are our first sight of the town of Devizes.

After what seems like eternity, but is actually only about a mile, the path reaches the rather splendid, new (1990) Coate Road Bridge.

The road going off left runs eventually to the small village of Coate. However, within about half a mile it passes an old clay farm that was once the source of some of the clay 'puddling' used in the construction of the canal.

After the navvies had dug the basic canal pit, it had to be lined in order to prevent water seepage and loss. Bed clay puddling was a mixture of gravel and clay that had been worked together to form a watertight 'puddle' or sealant. Gutter puddle, layered onto the sides of the canal, was more usually made of pure blue clay. In porous ground, the bed was given about eighteen inches of puddling and the sides about three feet. In poor draining soils they were able to get away with less puddling and in some cases the bottom wouldn't get any at all. In these cases only the sides were coated to prevent any sideways leakage that would weaken the bank.

Once laid, the puddling was worked into position and flattened (remember these were days before JCBs) by the feet of the navvies. On occasion cattle and sheep were herded over the clay in order to further consolidate the lining.

One of the rather unimportant consequences of the structure of the canal is that it is ill-advised for anyone to go punting. The pole either gets stuck in the puddling or, worse, it may actually go all the way through and cause a major leak. So don't do it!

The scenery is becoming progressively more urban (in a pleasant sort of way). The barracks now loom large on our right as we pass over a small inlet and into a cutting. The narrow dirt path now passes a housing estate high on the right-hand bank. After a second inlet we pass under Brickham Bridge. Houses are now on the right-hand bank and high trees on the left. The gardens of the houses come right down to the canal and several have mooring spaces. At least two were for sale should you fancy a move.

After a few more houses, the canal bends sharp right and under a main road bridge (the A361 again). A quick way to the eastern part of the town can be taken here by ascending to the road and turning left. Determined walkers will continue under the bridge and up to a newish, made-up pathway. There are now flats to the left and allotments to the right.

If Sherlock Homes took this route, he would undoubtedly conclude that the dog population of Devizes is both numerous and healthy. Watch your steps!

Otherwise Devizes is a pleasant, old-fashioned country town with all the facilities that you are likely to require. It was originally built around the Norman castle on a hill to the west of the modern centre (note that the present building is a Victorian folly and privately owned). The hub of the town now is the mostly eighteenth century Market Place. Here the town bustles and lives especially on Thursdays when the market takes place. Devizes church, Saint John's, is twelfth century.

Perhaps the most important building in Devizes is not the church or the castle, but the brewery. Devizes is home for the Wadworth company; the home of 6X. Pilgrims will find the site in Northgate Street (turn right at Town Bridge and you will find it before you reach Market Place). Wadworth is a family owned business which has been brewing in Devizes since 1875 (the current building was put up ten years later). It not only makes the much loved 6X but also IPA, Old Timer (a strong ale), Farmer's Glory and two keg beers; Northgate Bitter and Raker. Here in this one factory, 200 employees produce about twenty million pints a year. Imagine it. The company makes its own oak casks in which the beer undergoes its secondary fermentation and then distribution. This is real Real Ale. Interestingly, Henry Wadworth, the founder of the company, was the first man to cycle from London to Bath (it took him two and a half days). Let it not be said that this book isn't informative!

We still have a little way to go. Almost imperceptibly the towpath rises to reach the top of the next bridge, with the canal still languishing some twenty feet below. This is Park Road Bridge. The gated path on the right is known as Quaker's Walk.

Continue over the bridge. The buildings to the left are parts of Devizes Hospital. If you intend to stop in Devizes, veer right and take the lower of the two paths offered at this point. This will take you to the Devizes Wharf but no farther. If you do not wish to visit the wharf, take the high road because you will have to cross the next bridge as the towpath changes sides here. This bridge is Cemetery Road Bridge - there being a cemetery to the right (presumably you get a good view from the hospital wards). Pass under the bridge and out to the wharf.

Devizes Wharf (formerly called Town Wharf) is the only one remaining of three that were in the town at the height of K&A Canal activity. The area has been neatly 'touristed' and there is now a big car park, a cafe, a series of craft shops, a theatre, a WC, as well as the shop, museum and headquarters of the Kennet and Avon Canal Trust. The latter are housed in an old granary building (built c.1810) which became a bonded wine warehouse (where it awaited the attentions of the tax man) to our left as we enter the wharf area.

The K&A Canal Trust's contribution to the restoration of the canal has been pivotal and it cannot be overpraised for its activities on our behalf. From political pressure to fund raising, from education to manual labour;

its role has been a key factor in the success of the re-building of the waterway. There are now over 4,000 members and they've raised (and spent!) over £2½million. The trust produces its own magazine, The Butty, and holds numerous events of all sorts. On top of that, its members run the historic Crofton and Claverton pumping stations. Their aim has been to restore the canal as a public amenity for boaters, walkers, industrial archaeologists, fishermen, naturalists and picnickers alike. If you wish to contribute or join the trust, its address is; The Canal Centre, Couch Lane, Devizes, Wiltshire SN10 1EB (0380-722859).

The trust's museum (upstairs from the shop - small entrance fee) is well worth a look. It has some excellent, highly professional displays on the canal, the people who built it and the people who worked it.

Devizes is well stocked with shops and places to eat and drink (there are eighteen Wadworth's pubs alone). There isn't a BR station here (although at one time there was a branch line from Westbury to Trowbridge/ Bradford). There is, however, a range of buses. Some destinations are easier to get to than others but progress should be possible.

All the buses stop in the Market Place. From the trust's shop, walk alongside the old granary and up to Couch Lane. Cross the main road here and go along the interestingly named Snuff Street (those with good memories will recall that this road leads to the cemetery). Market Place will be found at the end of the street. Turn left for the bus stops and right for Wadworth's. Market Place is architecturally very interesting as most of the buildings date from the seventeenth and eighteenth centuries and have been little altered. This must have been what most town centres were like at the turn of the nineteenth century. If you want the tourist information office, turn left and bear right. It's on the right shortly thereafter.

6: THE K&A WALK
DEVIZES to BRADFORD-ON-AVON

Superficially quiet with terrific ends is the best way of summing up this stretch. At the beginning the canal path passes through the busy, old market town of Devizes and then on to the Caen Hill locks, one of the most celebrated wonders of the canal world. Here the industrial archaeologist and the photographer will wile away both the hours and the Kodachrome. From there the route returns to the rural idyll and calm of the Wiltshire countryside. We pass near the villages of Seend and Semington, both of which have seen canal related industrial activity in the past. After winding around the towns of Melksham and Trowbridge, we get our first hints of the glory of Bath when we first meet the River Avon and then enter the delightful town of Bradford-on-Avon.

Transport between Bradford and Devizes is not difficult - just awkward. Both towns are well supplied with buses and Bradford even has the delight of British Rail (gosh), but connecting the two places directly is not possible. Detours are therefore required. The half-hourly Badgerline 264 is firstly taken to Trowbridge. You then take the somewhat less frequent Trowbridge to Devizes bus (eg Melksham Coaches 77). I did it in one and a quarter hours so it's not speedy. It is arguably worth doing, however, for a tour of the Trowbridge one-way system in which a journey of 100 yards from the Town Hall to the Devizes road involves the circumnavigation of the entire town.

Devizes has a wide range of shops and is a good place to stock up with provisions (early closing is Wednesday). Seend and Semington have small village shops whilst Bradford has a slightly larger and very pleasant town centre. As before, the canal is within close proximity of pubs virtually all the way along.

A. DEVIZES to SEMINGTON

Distance: 6½ miles/11 kilometres

Map: OS Landranger 173 (Swindon, Devizes & surrounding area)

Transport: No bus goes to Semington from Devizes. If you wish to return to Devizes, you should first go either north to Melksham or south to Trowbridge by means of the Badgerline 234. Buses to Devizes can be had from either place. There is a direct route from Seend by means of the Melksham coach to/from Trowbridge (0225-704528). Sells Green can also be reached by means of the Bath bus (Badgerline 271, 272, or 273). Timetables for all the buses can be found at the bus stops in Devizes Market Place (near W.H.Smith and directly opposite on the other side of the road).

Car Parks: Devizes: Large car park at the wharf (well signposted) and others in town.
Marsh Lane, Foxhanger (bottom of Caen Hill): On-road
Seend & Semington: On-road parking
Semington Bridge: Small amount

If you're joining the route from the centre of Devizes, you should first make your way to the town wharf. From the Market Place, turn towards the brewery which is on the north side and cross to the right-hand side of the road. Turn right along Snuff Street and continue over New Park Street and into Couch Lane. There are numerous signposts directing you towards the wharf and the route is relatively straightforward. Once at the wharf, and after a visit to the Canal Trust Centre, return to Couch Lane, cross the canal at Cemetery Bridge and turn down left to continue the K&A Walk. A towpath sign is available to help find the route.

The towpath continues on this side for only a short distance. After Kennet Lock the path crosses back to the south bank at Devizes Town Bridge. If you turn left here, you can return via Northgate Street to the Market Place. Note that you don't have to cross the road in order to continue. After passing over the canal, turn left to have a look at the other side of Kennet Lock. You can then pass under the bridge using the small tunnel on this, south side, of the canal.

The towpath now passes through some built-up areas and this part of the path seems to be busy at virtually any time of the day at any time of the year. We pass three locks and the Black Horse public house before passing through a small tunnel under Prison Bridge.

To reach the Black Horse, walk across a footbridge which runs alongside Prison Bridge and then follow the road round to the right. The prison itself has long since disappeared. On the opposite side of the bridge is a plaque dedicated to the memory of John Blackwell. Blackwell was a resident

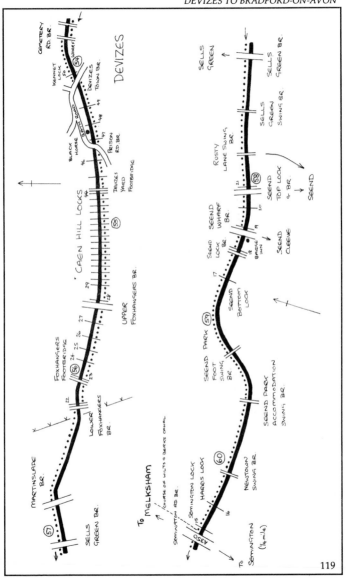

119

Caen Hill Flight, Devizes

engineer with the canal during its construction. He supervised the building of the Avon towpath and the Caen Hill locks, and worked for the company for thirty-four years. Interestingly Brunel (who had some dealings with him when a road was built in the valley between Limpley Stoke and Bath) described him as bigoted and obstinate. Luckily his employers didn't think this affected his work and here is his plaque to prove it. His son, Thomas, was also an engineer with the company.

The towpath is now a broad dirt track and passes two locks before reaching Devizes Yard and Sir Hugh Stockwell (Caen Hill Top) Lock.

We are now at the top of Caen Hill. The canal at Devizes is notable, not only for the home of the K&A Canal Trust, but also for the locks. For Devizes has twenty-nine of them, giving a total rise or fall of 237 feet over a distance of just two and a quarter miles. In front of us is the famous Caen Hill flight of sixteen locks which is one of the most spectacular features of Britain's inland waterway network. It is now an established tourist attraction and if you have arrived on a sunny Sunday, you will no doubt be surrounded by people.

If you stand by Sir Hugh Stockwell, you can see the problem faced by the canal engineers. The land to the west now drops steeply. It was John Rennie who decided to scale the hill in one flight. He built the sixteen locks here to lift the canal a total of 140 feet. The amount of work required to complete the locks was considerable and Caen Hill was both the last section to be completed in the original construction and the last part to be completed in the more recent restoration.

As you walk down, you will see that each lock is provided with its own reservoir in the shape of large side pounds, built like huge ponds on the northern side of the locks. These reservoirs are about six feet deep and each measures about forty-five yards by seventy. An extra supply of water to each lock is necessary because of the short pound space between the locks. Without these reservoirs, each pound would be completely drained every time the lock was used and passage would be stopped. With the reservoirs, the water level hardly moves and boats can use the locks freely.

The towpath down to Upper Foxhangers Bridge is a clear dirt track. It is possible to walk on the far side of the reservoir pounds for some part of the way. This can be done by crossing the canal at one of the locks. Walkers can also cross at Queen's Lock to read the inscription on the plinth (although this isn't as exciting as it sounds).

It was possible to use the K&A even before Caen Hill was opened. A horse-drawn railway was built to move goods from Foxhanger to the top of Caen Hill (a total of one and a half miles). Some traces of a railway embankment can be found in the undergrowth to the left of the towpath. It is also said that the train used to pass through the cute little tunnels that go under the bridges to the east of Caen Hill.

Canal users didn't have to put up with the inconvenience for long. On 28th December 1810 the locks were ready and opened for traffic. The first barge through was loaded with freestone (a fine-grained, easily-sawn limestone or sandstone) for the Earl of Ailesbury. A general opening was declared three days later on New Year's eve and two barges of coal ascended the locks, even though a third was trapped because of a heavy frost. Things got luxurious in 1829 when gas lights were fitted so that night passage was possible (although at extra cost).

It takes, depending on your dawdling, about thirty to forty minutes to walk up all twenty-nine locks from Lower Foxhangers Bridge to Kennet Lock. It takes the floating fraternity considerably longer! The best time I've seen is two and a half hours recorded by a 'Newbury trader' in the early part of this century. However, things gradually declined as the canal fell into disrepair. In 1929 a pleasure steamer, 'Gaiety', took five hours and by 1951 the whole flight was declared unsafe. As a consequence all the locks between Bradford and Devizes were padlocked and passage ceased. Certainly when I first came here in 1983, the whole flight was dry with broken lock gates and head-high weeds. An awful lot of work has gone on since then.

The flight was re-opened by the Queen on 8th August 1990 but sadly that doesn't mean that boats can now pass at will. Water supply to the top locks remains a problem, particularly after a couple of long dry summers. This situation will hopefully be remedied in the not so distant future.

As you walk down the hill don't ignore the sights to the left! Through the thick hedge is the clay pit where the canal company's brick works was established. The works produced bricks not only for these locks but also for other parts of the canal such as the Bruce Tunnel.

By the way, it's not that the locks don't have names just here, it's simply that there are so many of them I could fill a whole page with just that! Keep an eye out for the lock names because a number of them have been 'christened' after people or organisations who have assisted with the resurrection of the canal as a navigable concern.

At the bottom of Caen Hill the canal narrows and passes through lock 28. The towpath passes under Upper Foxhangers Bridge. A towpath sign points us in the direction of Semington.

The road to the right here is a popular on-road parking spot - it can get packed on Sundays. The house to the left just before the bridge is Foxhangers House. This was originally the superintendent engineer's house. It was later sold to a laundry. The washing water which drained into the canal below the bridge caused the water to foam and this point became popularly known as the soapy pound.

The muddy footpath now takes us to five locks in quick succession with four side pounds. On the left is Upper Foxhangers Farm and to the right, at the second lock after the bridge, Upper Foxhangers Cottages. By the time we reach the fourth lock, the farm to the left is Lower Foxhangers Farm and the cottages to the right Lower Foxhangers Cottages. The canal bends slightly left to another lock.

At Lower Foxhangers it is possible to take a public footpath right to the small village of Rowde. The footpath left goes to the main Trowbridge/Melksham to Devizes road (A365).

The last lock of the Devizes 29 is just after a gentle bend left. Enjoy it because you won't see another for two miles.

At the bridge follow the white arrow which directs you up to the bridge and across it. The towpath now uses the northern bank all the way to Avoncliff aqueduct.

Just before the canal bends right again and into the long straight Summerham cut, the Wiltshire, Somerset & Weymouth railway line used to cross at the now decapitated bridge. The line was opened (as a broad gauge line) in 1848 and joined the Pewsey-Westbury line to the Melksham-Bradford line. It was taken over by the GWR in 1850. If opened today, it would have made a very useful return ride back from Bradford to Devizes. But, alas and alack, decisions to close railway lines aren't made on the basis that people might wish to actually use them.

After playing host to a number of boats moored around the railway bridge, the canal now takes a straight cut. About one third of the way along, the canal passes over the Summerham Brook via an aqueduct. The precise point can be seen where the brook passes under the railway embankment to the right of the canal. Within quarter of a mile the path passes over a concrete bridge bringing a small stream in from the right.

The seemingly insignificant little stream is actually quite important. This is the Seend feeder and is the only supply of water to the canal between Devizes and Claverton.

At Martinslade Wharf two ramshackle, corrugated iron buildings on the right (a timberyard) are followed by Martinslade Bridge. Shortly thereafter, we pass under Sells Green Bridge. Turn right at either bridge to visit the small village of Sells Green and the Three Magpies pub.

After passing by two swing bridges (Sells Green and then Rusty Lane), the path meets Seend Top Lock (21) and Seend Selver Bridge.

Turn left at the bridge to visit Seend village which has both the Bell Inn and a bus to Devizes and/or Trowbridge. Back in the days of Henry VII, Seend was a famous weaving village (a group of Flemish weavers settled here in the seventeenth century) and John Aubrey described the Seend of 1684 as containing 'many well-built houses'. It still does, in fact, as visitors or those bus-riders returning via Trowbridge will attest.

Non-visitors pass to the right of the bridge, over the road via two stiles and then back to the canal again. Within 150 yards we reach Seend Lock 20.

The scene at lock 20 appears so tranquil and calm that it's impossible

The Barge Inn, Seend Cleeve

to believe that this was once a hive of industry. Seend Hill, or Ridge, to our left (about quarter of a mile west of the village itself) is composed of limestone with a layer of greensand on top. In the nineteenth century, this was the site of a major discovery of ironstone. In the 1870s 300 men worked here producing some 300 tons of iron a week.

In the early days the ore was simply dug and shipped by canal to the South Wales blast furnaces. Later the Great Western Iron Ore Smelting Company built two blast furnaces on site and constructed a tramway to link the quarry with the canal (and then to the railway just to the north). The high cost of doing this soon ruined the quarry company and it was declared bankrupt in 1859. Two years later the Wiltshire Iron Company took over. A triumph of hope over experience perhaps because this company was also wound up after just seven years trading. Despite this, work continued until 1889 when the furnaces were demolished and things ground to a complete halt. In 1905 the Westbury & Seend Ore & Oxide Company bought the quarry. Further activity was stimulated by the First World War but everything stopped shortly thereafter.

Apparently, there's still quite a lot of low-grade iron ore left so if you fancy having a go, this could be your big opportunity. However, don't get too excited. The site of the quarry on Seend Ridge is now a Site of Special Scientific (Geological) Interest so it's likely that they wouldn't let you do it.

The path bends slightly right and up to Seend Lock 19 and, shortly thereafter, Seend Wharf Bridge. Here on the left, after the bridge, is another Barge Inn (and there are still more to come). To reach this one you'll have to go up to the bridge and across the canal. Alternatively, turn left at Seend Lock Bridge into Seend Cleeve for the competition (the Brewery Inn) in about quarter of a mile.

The path now passes Seend Bottom Lock (18) and a patchwork bridge (cross stile here). Within a short distance along a dirt path, we meet the last Seend Lock (17) before bending left to Seend Park Foot Swing Bridge. A public footpath right here goes to Melksham.

As you pass up the oppotunity to visit Melksham, you should perhaps spare a thought for the place. The original route for the K&A (ie. the canal section that joined the Avon Navigation at Bath to the Kennet Navigation at Newbury) went through Melksham. The actual route was : Bath - Bradford - Melksham - Lacock - Chippenham - Calne - Marlborough - Ramsbury - Hungerford - Newbury. This route, of course, is mostly much farther north than the K&A as built. Indeed, the section between Melksham and Chippenham would have gone due north for just over six miles before turning suddenly east towards Calne. John Whitworth of the Thames & Severn Canal criticised the route saying that there would be problems with water availabilty. However, John Rennie made his first survey and recommended the route to a meeting of the canal committee in November1790.

By July 1793 Rennie had changed his mind. After a second survey he recommended the more southerly route via Great Bedwyn and Devizes. He'd decided that Whitworth was right after all - water supply at the summit would be a problem. The new route would not be so cursed. The revised route was mostly as built but included the proposal for the canal to pass through Trowbridge before turning north-west towards Bradford. Melksham, Chippenham and Calne were to be served by the Wiltshire & Berkshire Canal (see later) and Marlborough was to have a branch 'line' from the K&A (which it never, in fact, got). In the end, Trowbridge also lost out. In an effort to save funds, the town was by-passed; saving two miles and the cost of a lengthy aqueduct.

The canal now bends back right to Seend Park Accommodation Swing Bridge. The farm to the left is Seend Park Farm and the stream that winds around it is Semington Brook. After 100 yards the path passes a demolished swing bridge and then onto an intact one at Newtown, which has Newtown farmhouse to its right.

At this point the towpath deteriorates into a very squelchy track - possibly the muddiest part of the entire K&A Walk! Within 200 yards we pass Harris Lock.

Near Harris Lock is a covered dry dock with its natty horse weather vane. The dock is one of only two on the entire canal. The village in the distance is Semington.

Shortly after Harris Lock the path is squeezed between two lengths of rusty white metal fencing. After passing through some overgrown bushes, there is a slight indentation in the canal and a handsome house with a healthy looking vegetable plot and a yard on the right-hand side.

The towpath here actually crosses over a bricked-up bridge, for at this point the Wiltshire and Berkshire Canal once joined the K&A. The canal ran from Semington Bridge due north (through the vegetable plot and the yard and alongside the road) and up to Melksham. The building to the left of the former canal was the toll collector's cottage (now a private house). The W&B ran via Melksham, Lacock and Swindon to Abingdon where it joined the Thames - a total distance of fifty-two miles and one furlong (in old money).

Building work on the W&B started about the same time as the K&A - in 1795 - and was finished just before - in September 1810 (the section from Semington to Swindon was finished in 1804). When the builders reached the Thames, there were great celebrations - seemingly helped along with 'many appropriate toasts and songs'. The canal was an important conduit for Somerset coal. In 1840 some 56,000 tons were shipped north from the K&A. Despite this quite active trade, the K&A company was always suspicious of the W&B. It feared loss of trade by means of a sneaky back route from Bristol to London. As it happens, of course, the trade found the alternative route by opting for the railways and so both lost out.

As you can see, over the years the W&B has fared the worst of the two canals. After closure in 1914, most of the sections have dried out (although some do fill in after heavy rain) and in many places (like here) it has simply disappeared altogether. This hasn't stopped the ever-hopeful canal enthusiast from dreaming of a re-opened W&B but progress will be very hard.

The bridge that we meet almost immediately is Semington Road Bridge and the end of this half section. The footbridge across the canal here is on the far (western) side of the bridge. Turn left for Semington village.

Semington village is straightforward rather than picturesque. It is notable, however, for our first Cotswold stone houses; reminding us perhaps that we are just fifteen miles from the centre of Bath (a fraction over sixty from the Thames). The Somerset Arms public house (which also does accommodation) and then the local post office-cum-village shop can be found on the right-hand side of the road after about quarter of a mile (don't expect Sainsbury's). The bus stop is just outside the Somerset Arms. Buses go north-south (Melksham-Trowbridge).

B. SEMINGTON to BRADFORD-ON-AVON

Distance:	5¹/₂ miles/9 kilometres
Map:	OS Landranger 173 (Swindon, Devizes & surrounding area)
Transport:	There is no direct link between Semington and Bradford. Those wishing to return from Bradford should take the frequently running bus to Trowbridge and then the Trowbridge-Chippenham bus that passes through Semington. All buses in Trowbridge stop and start at the Town Hall.
Car Parks:	Semington and Hilperton: Limited on-road
	Bradford-on-Avon: Signposted car parks in town

If you are coming from Semington village, turn north along the A350 in the direction of Melksham and walk for about quarter of a mile until you reach the Semington Road Bridge that crosses the canal. There is a footbridge on the left (western) side. Cross the bridge and turn left to pass down to the canal. Here a towpath sign points us in the direction of Hilperton. It doesn't say so, but it's about two and a half miles.

After just one hundred yards the canal bends left. Here Semington Brook (big enough to be more properly called a thriving stream) passes under the canal. John Rennie's answer was the Semington

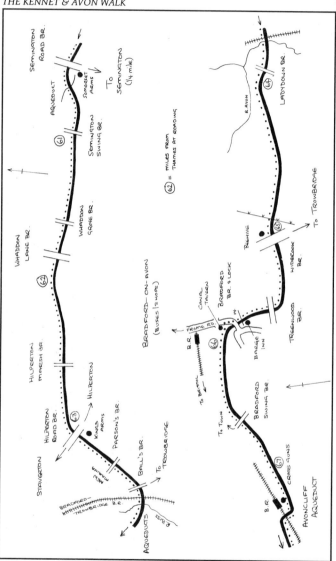

Aqueduct, a fine structure and the first of three between here and Bradford.

This is perhaps a good point at which to say some more about John Rennie, the principal engineer of the K&A Canal. Born in East Lothian in 1761, Rennie, at twenty-nine could have been considered somewhat of a rash choice to survey and build the canal. After all, there was big money at stake. There were murmurings that they should have got someone with more experience but in the opinion of many, Rennie turned out to be one of the four great canal builders (the other three being William Jessop, Thomas Telford and, perhaps the greatest of all, James Brindley).

Rennie started his working life in the same way as Brindley, as an apprentice millwright (ie. someone who designs and builds mills). But, after a classical education at Edinburgh University, he began to find his reputation as a civil engineer. The Kennet & Avon Canal was only the first. At roughly the same time (1792) he became responsible for the Lancaster Canal which ran forty-two and a half miles from near Wigan up to Kendal. He also designed the docks at London, Liverpool, Leith, Dublin and Hull; constructed Plymouth breakwater; and drained the fens. But perhaps his most famous designs were for bridges. It was Rennie who built the old Waterloo and Southwark bridges and, perhaps the most famous of all, the granite London Bridge. This bridge, the construction of which had to be supervised by his son (for Rennie died in 1821 and the bridge opened in 1831), is the one that now stands, somewhat incongruously, in the Arizona desert. You can only imagine what he would have thought of that.

The path continues with the outskirts of Semington on the left-hand bank. Should you wish to revisit the village, you could cross at the Semington Swing Bridge that we now pass. After going under some power lines, the canal enters one of its quietest phases and probes into deep, peaceful country.

My notes on this section say that there's nothing here but cows, grass and crows. Even the coots had temporarily deserted the scene. This is deeply pastoral and a wonderful place to be on a warm summer's day. A bit dodgy in the cold, windy autumn but great in summer, I expect.

The path passes under Whaddon Grove Bridge and, after a further 200 yards, the new-ish Whaddon Lane Bridge. The towpath now becomes a quite luxurious, firm and dry, made-up path. Whilst

Bath Top Lock

still within sight of the bridge, the towpath notches up its one hundredth kilometre since the Thames. Ignoring this kilometre-stone, we continue through open county and pass a former bridge before reaching Hilperton Marsh Bridge where a track to the left goes to Hilperton Marsh Farm.

The factory with the tall, shiny chimney over to the right is the Nestlé works at Staverton. Initially a condensed milk factory, the plant is now involved in food processing generally. The site formerly had a series of woollen and clothing factories on it. The original factory, which employed some 1,500 people, was burnt down (some say under suspicious circumstances) in 1824. The works was rebuilt with power looms - apparently the first in this part of the world. Contrary to expectations (mine at least), Nestlé aren't recent purchasers. They've actually been here since 1898. Since then they've grown to be the biggest food company in the world.

The canal now turns right alongside some des. res. on the left-hand bank. At Marsh Wharf it passes under Hilperton Road Bridge. Turn left here for the Kings Arms (a full fifty yards away). Alternatively turn right for the Old Bear Inn at Staverton (slightly farther). We are now three miles from the centre of Bradford-on-Avon.

The wharf at Hilperton Marsh Bridge was used to unload goods for Trowbridge, which was not only by-passed by the K&A but never even got its own branch line - shame.

Continue along the good path and then up and over a new stone bridge.

This straight half mile stretch is crammed with 'parked' boats. On the left is Hilperton Marina (operated by the Kennet & Avon Navigation Company). Its huge modern shop and service building looms over the canal, looking as if it plucks customers from the water like a heron catching fish. On the right, all is new. It will no doubt be completely different when you pass it. When I went this way, a muddy patch with abundant mooring space had (confusingly) two labels; 'Staverton New Marina' and 'Avonmore'. Whatever it's called, the development is clearly aimed at the prosperous boater. The mooring places are all a mere pebble-shot (an up-market form of stone's throw) from the 'waterside development' of luxury one bedroom apartments, luxury two, three or four bedroom houses, luxury hotel and luxury restaurant. All a sure indication that the function of the canal is no longer as a commercial waterway but strictly a leisure-time cruiseway. Well, at least something's happening, I suppose. And the moored barges do look pretty. And it is a nice footbridge.

The good path now lets us down. We're back to a muddy, grass track. We pass under the new bridge which connects Staverton New Marina/Avonmere with the outside world.

There is now an aging industrial estate on the left (south) bank. We pass under Ball's Bridge where a towpath sign promises Bradford. The public footpath to the right wanders off to Staverton. The one to the left (over the bridge) steps firmly in the direction of Trowbridge, the centre of which is now just three-quarters of a mile south.

Trowbridge is a reasonably big town with all the shops and facilities one would expect, including accommodation, buses and trains. As mentioned before, the one-way system is worth experiencing but the centre is largely pedestrianised and quite pleasant. All the buses leave from the town hall (well signposted).

Meanwhile, the canal continues its journey west and passes over two aqueducts.

The Ladydown and Biss Aqueducts are both splendid structures. Chronologically, the Biss Aqueduct (the second one that runs over the River Biss) was built first - in fact, when the canal was constructed in 1798. By 1803 the structure was already in a bad state of repair because the poor quality stone that was used to build it was beginning to crumble. It was rebuilt using better grade material from the Bathampton quarry. The Ladydown railway aqueduct was built some 40-odd years later when the Trowbridge to Chippenham and Bradford Railway line (originally part of the independent Wiltshire, Somerset & Weymouth Railway) was installed. Both aqueducts can be best viewed by a little bit of trespass which, of course, I won't recommend.

A sign at this point, incidentally, says that the fishing rights are the property of the Airsprung AA.

The route now bends gently right and then left. Within half a mile, a river can be seen down right.

The land to the right drops away dramatically. The river in the valley bottom (just beyond the rather ugly elevated pipeline) is the River Biss.

The track now improves to a solid made-up path. Just before the next bridge, Ladydown Bridge, two routes are offered. Softies can continue right along the good path, canal-huggers (and under-bridge graffiti addicts) will want to take the grass track that passes underneath the bridge. The two paths rejoin shortly after the bridge.

On the southern (left-hand) side a fine, long double row of poplar trees stands over the canal. To the right, through the dense foliage of the oaks, a river can be seen.

The Biss has joined the River Avon, which will now entwine itself around the canal right the way to Bath. This version of the Avon has risen near Badminton Park (yes, the one that runs the horse trials) and passed a rather circuitous route through Malmesbury, Chippenham and Melksham before joining us on the way to Bradford. Those with keen long sight will be able to follow the course of the river as it winds its way through the meadows and up to the town which can now be seen in the distance (about one and three-quarter miles away). The TV mast directly ahead is at Lye Green just to the south-west of Bradford.

After a deep indentation on the left-hand bank, the canal bends right to a straight section leading to the outskirts of Bradford. The right-hand hedge is swathed in old man's beard. Shortly after passing under some power cables, there is a marina on the southern side of the canal. This is Widbrook.

Widbrook was to be the point where the Dorset & Somerset Canal joined the K&A. The D&S as planned ran for forty-eight miles from near Blandford via Wincanton and Frome to here. The work started in 1796 but by 1803 all the money had gone with just a short section left to complete. The rapid use of money, the call for more and the political situation had scared the investors. Sadly no further funds could be raised and the canal was never opened.

Such problems seem to be endemic within these great construction works. The K&A was certainly no exception. With the help of Kenneth Clew's excellent history of the canal, we glean the following points which bear comparison with a certain twentieth century tunnel project.

The canal (ie. the stretch from Newbury to Bath) was foreseen by a small group of keen, influential men in the 1780s. In 1790 the cost was estimated at just over £210,000. Initially there wasn't a lot of enthusiasm but canal mania took hold and subscriptions poured in. The project was launched and an Act of Parliament sought.

Reverberations from the French Revolution led to a general financial crisis. As a result, by 1793 the cost estimate rose to £377,000. Despite this, building work started in 1794 albeit with cost-saving measures being put immediately into operation. This meant that proper surveys weren't done and higher costs resulted as builders fought their way through unexpectedly tough ground. Local contractors found that they couldn't achieve what they had promised. There were large rises in costs and completion dates weren't met.

In 1796 shareholders began to default. Work on the middle section was postponed. Work on the western section was held up for nine months in 1798 because of the 'wetness of the season'. Financial problems meant that in March 1799, the company had to order that no new work be started until further notice. In addition, there were problems with the work already done; some parts had collapsed and needed re-building. Luckily the open canal sections were beginning to earn money and a new share issue contributed some urgently needed cash. But the problems continued.

In 1805 Parliament allowed the company to seek £200,000 above and beyond that already asked for. However, the shares weren't snapped up. The public had lost interest. But by some clever financial dealing, the company continued and on the last day of December 1810, the canal was completed. There was little rejoicing and the final bill was £979,314 (including £100,000 for the purchase of the Kennet Navigation), over four times the original estimate.

As I walked this section, the financial situation of the tunnel building company was being revived, after a dodgy period of complex negotiation, and the public's view of the whole affair had turned cynical. Still if history does repeat itself, as we are often told, the Channel tunnel should be a great success - or at least until its equivalent of the railway turns up to supersede it.

The towpath has now reached the outskirts of Bradford-on-Avon. After passing a toll point, the canal passes under Widbrook Bridge.

Pass to the right of the bridge and up to the road should you wish to visit the Beehive pub. If you are seeking a short route to the centre of town, it is quicker to turn right along the road here but not much.

The good path continues into a leafy cutting.

Notable amongst the shrubbery here was a beautiful deep, rich purple tree mallow and a walnut tree (no nuts).

As the canal passes a trading estate on the far side, it bends sharply northwards and passes under Treenwood Bridge. There is now an unattractive yard on the right and some houses on the left.

When they were building the canal, the area to the north of the yard was the Bradford clay 'farm'; another source of puddling clay similar to that from Coate just before Devizes.

Within a couple of hundred yards yet another Barge Inn is found on the far bank and this heralds the start of Bradford Upper Wharf (or Frome Road Wharf).

The first cuts on the western section of the new K&A Canal were made here in October 1794. There were two wharves at Bradford; this one and the lower wharf just over the other side of the bridge. As you can see there is a slipway and a dry dock here (in case you're wondering where the water drains to, there is a specially constructed culvert to a point just the other side of the lock). The dry dock was previously used as a gauging station where barges could be tested for their carrying capacity and tolls calculated.

The small stone building, formerly the wharfinger's house, is now home to the K&A Canal Trust shop (open weekends) and WCs. The wharfinger was responsible for collecting the tolls, as well as supervising the wharf and lock. The wharf is also the home of the Trust's narrow boat 'Ladywood' which offers trips on Sundays and Bank Holidays.

This section of the walk is completed by passing the lock and going up to the Bradford-on-Avon (Frome Road) Bridge. Turn right here for the BR station and the centre of town (quarter of a mile). If you wish to continue on the towpath, turn right at the bridge and then left just before and alongside the Canal Tavern (well signposted). There is no towpath under the bridge.

Bradford-on-Avon Lock is the only one in this half-section. It was once notable for being the deepest lock on the whole canal with a rise/fall of 10'3" (for comparison the Devizes Locks are generally about 6'6" and the Seend Locks about 7-8'). Since its restoration in the 1970s, the record now goes to the suitably named Bath Deep Lock (amalgamated locks 8 and 9) with a rise/fall of 18'8".

Bradford-on-Avon was once a very important wool town and the wharf must have seen load after load of cloth shipped off to markets around the country. In 1800 there were over thirty factories here, mostly producing a characteristic heavy woollen cloth. Some of the mill buildings can still be seen high on the northern hill. By the middle of the nineteenth century, the weaving industry was all but gone in the face of competition from the great mills of northern England.

What the woollen wealth left is a splendid town with some wonderful buildings and a delightful, steep-sided, town centre. At the heart of the

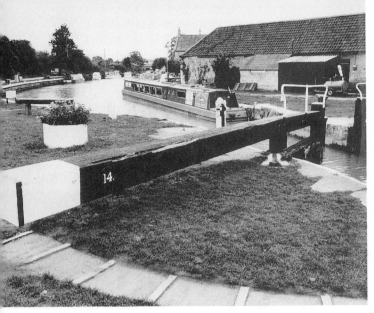

Bradford-on-Avon lock and wharf

town is the famous fourteenth century Oratory Bridge over the River Avon. Perched, somewhat delicately, at one end of the bridge is a small enclosed, domed chapel dedicated to Saint Nicholas. In the seventeenth century the chapel was heartlessly converted into a small gaol where villains could be held for minor misdemeanours. The preacher John Wesley is said to have been locked up there for a night in 1757 after annoying the locals. The copper-coloured fish which bedecks the weather vane on top of the chapel/prison is (according to John Timson in the fascinating 'Timson's England') a gudgeon; a fish that was Saint Nicholas' emblem. You can probably amaze your companions with that one.

If you pass over the bridge and turn left along Church Street, you will also see the Saxon church founded in the eighth century. The centre has plenty of tourists without having been ruined. There is also a number of shops and pleasant watering places, as well as a regular supply of buses. In particular there is a good service that connects Bradford with both Bath and Trowbridge. The railway station is just off the Frome Road and, again, offers connections to Bath and Trowbridge.

✳   ✳   ✳

Tithe Barn, Bradford-on-Avon

7: THE K&A WALK
BRADFORD-ON-AVON to BATH

If you were to be swished away to the proverbial desert island and the interviewer allowed you to take only one section of the K&A Walk with you, this would have to be it. (And this volume would, of course, be your book!). These ten miles, between Bradford and Bath, make wonderful walking. At the start of the section is the delightful town of Bradford-on-Avon and then, pulling us all the way along, the wonder of Bath. Throughout the journey there's an almost unhealthy concentration of canal interest and great scenery. What more could you need?

The canal along this stretch has some of its finest structures and a large number of its most interesting places. The Avoncliff and Dundas Aqueducts are wonders of the Canal Age. The Claverton Pumping Station is a wonder of any age. And, as the canal weaves its way around and into the heart of Bath, there is a terrific combination of history, geography and incident. At Bath, with the passing of Widcombe Bottom Lock and Dolmeads Bridge, the K&A Canal of 1794-1810 finishes and the canal joins the River Avon to become the Avon Navigation. From there, there are just seventeen miles to the floating harbour at Bristol.

This section between Bath and Bradford is almost overflowing with public transport. It's regular and even runs on Sundays! We haven't seen such luxury since Newbury. BR has a regular service between Bath and Bradford, some of which stops at Avoncliff. The bus service between the two places is half-hourly during the week, but only two-hourly and then in the afternoons on Sundays. Sunday-car-linked strollers will therefore have to walk away from their vehicle and catch the bus back.

There are plenty of pubs at both ends and at convenient spots along the route. Bradford-on-Avon is a good place to stock up with provisions (early closing is Wednesday). Bath, of course, is one of the premier shopping centres in this part of the country.

Don't rush it, savour it.

A. BRADFORD-ON-AVON to DUNDAS AQUEDUCT

Distance:	4 miles/6½ kilometres
Map:	OS Landranger 173 (Swindon, Devizes & surrounding area)
	OS Landranger 172 (Bristol, Bath & surrounding area)
Transport:	BR: Bath-Bradford occasionally stops at Avoncliff.
	Enquiries to 0225-463075
	Bus: Badgerline 264 & 265 from Bath stops at the Avon Bridge in Bradford, the Viaduct Hotel which is near the Aqueduct (ask driver for best stop) and near Limpley Stoke Bridge. Enquiries to: 0225-464446.
Car Parks:	Bradford: Car parking at the railway station and in town
	Avoncliff: Very small car park at BR station
	Limpley Stoke Bridge: Off-road parking on western side
	Dundas: Lay-by on A36
Tourist Info:	Bradford on 02216-5797
	Bath on 0225-462831

If you're joining the route from the BR station at Bradford-on-Avon or from the centre of town, you should first make your way to the canal by turning right along Frome Road and walking quarter of a mile until you reach the Canal Tavern (which is on the right-hand side). If you reach the bridge that passes over the canal and the lock, you've gone too far. The towpath passes down a passageway on the bridge side of the Canal Tavern. When you reach the canal, turn right to continue the walk along a firm gravel path.

The Canal Tavern dates from the seventeenth century and was once used to stable the barge horses. I visited the place and the smell's definitely gone. The towpath at the back of the tavern was the site of Bradford Lower Wharf. One local guide book says that snuff was unloaded here and that the people of the town were once called 'snuffies' because all the shops and offices had a jar of the stuff for use by their customers. Clearly a story which is not to be sneezed at.

The canal now bends sharply left and passes a park (Victory Field) on the right. At the end of the park on the right is a tithe barn. A footpath to the left of the barn goes down to the River Avon and thence to the railway station and the centre of town. A towpath sign here points towards Avoncliff.

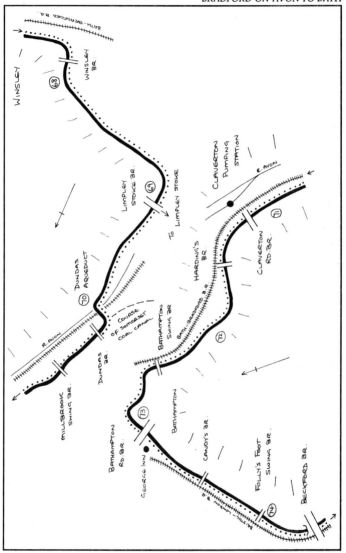

BATH - BRADFORD B.A.

WINSLEY

WINSLEY BR.

68

CLAVERTON PUMPING STATION

R. AVON

LIMPLEY STOKE BR.

69

TO LIMPLEY STOKE

71

CLAVERTON RD. BR.

DUNDAS AQUEDUCT

70

COURSE OF SOMERSET COAL CANAL

HARDING'S BR.

BATHAMPTON SWING BR.

BATH-BRADFORD B.R.

72

R. AVON

MILLBROOK SWING BR.

DUNDAS BR.

BATHAMPTON

73

BATHAMPTON BR.

CANDY'S BR.

FOLLY'S FOOT SWING BR.

BECKFORD BR.

BATHAMPTON RD. BR.

GEORGE INN

BRISTOL - WESTON B.R.

74

The early fourteenth century barn is a fine structure. Tithe barns were built to house the produce given to the church by the local farmers. The tithe was a tax of about 10% on all local produce and was taken to fund the church and the clergy. It could be given either as cash or more likely in kind as grain or fruit or whatever. As this is one of the biggest tithe barns in the entire country, it is quite clear that the local clergy did well by it. Certainly the building itself is comparatively huge with massive timber joists and a lovely stone-tiled roof. Of course, if it had been situated closer to London it would have been sold ages ago and converted into yuppie housing.

Just after the barn look back and down through the trees to the River Avon where Bradford's other ancient bridge, Barton Bridge, can be seen. The area on the right is the Wiltshire Council's Barton Farm Country Park.

The canal now curves away from the railway and the River Avon and passes Bradford-on-Avon Swing Bridge. The tarmac path joining from the right goes to Barton Park and the centre of town. Pass through a gate. (Here the nose detects the sewage works on the opposite bank). With the wooded hill to the left (Becky Addy Wood), the towpath reaches the outskirts of Avoncliff in approximately half a mile.

Becky Addy Wood was once the site of a stone quarry. Stone was removed by means of a tramway which ran down the hill and across the Avoncliff Aqueduct.

The first indication that you've reached Avoncliff is the noise coming from the River Avon weir down to your right. Pretty soon you meet some houses, then a chimney (a former flock mill) and the canal shop. The canal then sweeps suddenly right to the Avoncliff Aqueduct.

Avoncliff Aqueduct is the first of two along this section of the canal. The original plan was to put it on the Bradford side of the mills but Rennie decided to go downstream because the valley was narrower at this point. It is a huge structure, built originally of Bath stone, which was started in March 1796 and finished in late 1798. This was one of the original structures that started to crumble early in the life of the canal because of the low-grade stone that was used. As a result, much of the bridge has been patched with brick and, like many teeth, the original structure now relies on filling to hold it together. In the 1980s the restorers pressure-filled all the cracks with cement and completely re-worked the functional parts at the top. This means that the slight sag seen in the centre of the span isn't as serious as it looks and that from the top you might well think that it's a converted motorway bridge.

The railway was put into position some fifty-nine years after the completion of the main aqueduct. The structure was then extended with a slightly less flamboyant design at the other end near the present BR car park. Here you can see that the canal broadens slightly after passing over Rennie's section and then narrows again before turning left. This narrow, brick-wall sided portion passes directly over the line. It's said that during very cold weather, icicles used to dangle from the ceiling of the aqueduct like huge stalactites. Once really hardened, these could become quite dangerous to passing train traffic and special icicle removers were employed to knock them off every morning.

Continue across the aqueduct on this side for views and the BR station (unmanned). A footpath continues straight on and up the hill to Winsley village.

To continue the K&A Walk, turn right down the slope just before the aqueduct (on the Bradford side). On the right is the Canal Bookshop and the Cross Guns public house. After about five to ten yards turn left and carry on down alongside the aqueduct (use this opportunity to observe the famous sag). Immediately after, go up some steps on the left and continue round left to reach the western side of the aqueduct. Here on the right is Teazel's Coffee House and on the left a towpath sign indicating Dundas. Pass over the aqueduct (three-quarters of the way along is an information notice) and turn left at the end to follow the canal on its southern bank.

The canal now stands high on the side of Winsley Hill and looks down through the trees to the River Avon on the left. The sides of the canal at this point and for some distance on are made of stone and concrete. This rather drastic action was taken because this part of the canal is prone to 'blowouts'.

In fact, this whole section through to Limpley Stoke is puddled in a very different way to the rest of the canal. Instead of the original puddling clay, this stretch was firstly lined with polythene and then covered with concrete. This action was forced upon the restorers (the K&A Trust, the British Waterways Board and Wiltshire Council) following numerous problems with leakage and subsidence. The problems along here were so great that the whole section remained dry from 1954 right through to the early eighties. With the installation of the new plastic and concrete puddling and these strengthened walls, it is hoped that such slippage will be at least less frequent.

Because of the frequency of the blowouts, actions were taken to minimise the effects of any sudden loss of water and to isolate areas so that repairs could be made speedily. All along this stretch, the company installed emergency stop-gates (eighteen in just seven and a half miles of canal). Thus a portion of the canal can be separated off and repaired in the quickest time possible and with a minimal loss of precious water. Nowadays these have been largely replaced by the stop planks system that we've seen before, but stop-gates are still in position on either side of the Dundas aqueduct.

Mostly the blowouts were frustrating and time-consuming but sometimes they threatened life. When the canal was being built seven acres of land came down in one slip near Bradford. In January 1902 ten yards of canal bank sank. A group of workmen had only just got out of their boat before it disappeared down to the Avon. Thankfully nobody was hurt.

The reason for the problems relates entirely to the geology of the surrounding hills. The hillside here is made of oolite (a form of limestone) and it contains a number of fissures. This means that rain can readily permeate into the rock and force air upwards under pressure. Such pressure can become intense eventually forcing a means of escape out and down into the valley, thereby causing a landslip.

Continue along the relatively straight portion of the canal for about 200 yards.

In amongst the dense undergrowth to the left (down the slope in the direction of the railway) is Avoncliff Stone Wharf. It looks like a pile of overgrown junk now, but here stone from Becky Addy Wood was unloaded from the railway, dressed and loaded onto barges.

The canal sweeps sharply right and comes to Winsley Bridge, which we pass by going up to the side and down.

Turn right over Winsley Bridge and immediately left along a public footpath (up the steep hill) for the village of Winsley. Winsley is a pleasant village with a pub (the Seven Stars) and a shop. Whether it's worth the not-inconsiderable hike up the hill is, however, debatable. During the First World War, wounded soldiers at a special hospital in the village were given boat trips along the canal using the horse-drawn, narrowboat Bittern. This had been bought for the purpose by the Red Cross. Days out normally involved a trip to Bradford and back.

The hills here are blessed with two layers of the oolithic limestone that is the typical Bath stone. The lower layer is an inferior rock, whilst the upper layer is appropriately called the great oolitic limestone. At a point just after the canal turns gently left, Murhill Quary Wharf once stood. The wharf was connected to the Winsley stone quarries by means of a tramway which brought the good quality stone down from the hill above. Opened in 1803, the quarry was closed in the 1830s.

Just a bit farther along there are some nice houses on the right bank. Whilst the author was passing, the burglar alarm of the one directly on the canal was ringing, and the garden was being feverishly searched by two policemen (at least I assume they were). Not many country walks offer such interest.

The path continues along a relatively straight course for approximately three-quarters of a mile.

The canal is now enveloped in thick woodland and the dappled sunlight assists with the restful and peaceful ambience. The view to the left is mostly obscured but every now and again we get glimpses of the River Avon. To the right there is thick woodland (Murhill Wood).

The canal now curves sharply right to follow the contours around the hill at Limpley Stoke. Almost immediately, the canal passes under Limpley Stoke Bridge.

Shortly after the bend and before the bridge, keep an eye open left (through the hedge) for Fordside Tea Garden with its excellent ham sandwiches. At the bridge you could turn right for Winsley or left for Limpley Stoke if the mood takes you.

To reach Limpley Stoke, cross both the River Avon and the railway to reach the main road. Turn left to visit the village centre. The village has a small shop and the Hop Pole public house. There is also a route along the minor road back to Freshford, where there is an unmanned railway station with occasional trains to Bath or Bradford. Turn right at the Hop Pole to reach the A36 (Bath to Warminster road).

There is room for a few cars on the road on the western (left-hand) side. This bridge is also used by the Bath to Bradford-on-Avon bus.

Continue under the bridge and along the canal which now points roughly north. The view left clears and you should be able to see the Viaduct Hotel and some boats moored in the Bath And Dundas Canal Co. Marina.

Shortly after a wall there is a small bungalow and a derelict building (formerly a lengthsmen's cottage and barge horse stablings

Dundas Aqueduct

respectively) on the left. Here the canal passes through a stop gate. On the right bank there is a motley collection of wooden huts (formerly the end point for the Conkwell quarry railway). Here the canal turns left to pass over the Dundas Aqueduct.

Dundas Aqueduct is situated in Monkton Combe and enables the canal to pass from one side of the valley to the other before swinging west and into Bath. The aqueduct is, of course, named after Charles Dundas, the first chairman of the K&A company (to remind yourself re-read the section for Newbury to Hungerford). Memorial tablets to both Dundas and to John Thomas, a superintendent of works, were put onto the aqueduct in 1838.

Building work started at Monkton Combe in August 1796, right in the middle of both a financial and a stone crisis for the K&A company. The stone crisis resulted from the decision to use Bath stone from the company's own quarries for many of these structures. Rennie was against the idea. He wanted to use the more reliable brick but the company had its way. Conkwell quarry, conveniently situated at the eastern end of the aqueduct, is a good example of a working that harvested poor quality oolite which soon crumbled when weathered. As a consequence the aqueduct wasn't opened until 1805. Despite the delay, it is a splendid structure. The original had three arches and measured 150 feet long. When the railway was opened, a further section was added at the western end, although (as at Avoncliff) this was not incorporated into Rennie's original bridge.

Like the Avoncliff Aqueduct, the ravages of time have caused problems with the structure and those problems have been solved in a similar way using thoroughly modern methods. The renewed aqueduct was re-opened with suitable ceremony in July 1984 and now looks in good repair.

Pass over the aqueduct (half way across you pass from Wiltshire into Avon) and bear left to a small footbridge.

At this point a waterway enters the K&A from the left. This is now the mooring for a number of boats under the auspices of the Bath and Dundas Canal Company but was at one time the junction point with the Somerset Coal Canal.

The SCC was once an important raison d'être for the existence of the K&A at this end. The extraction and movement of coal from the thirty or so collieries in the Somerset field provided the K&A with a lot of trade - some 138,000 tonnes in 1838 alone. The canal ran from here to Midford where it split; one fork going to Timsbury (near Paulton) via Combe Hay and Dunkerton (a total of ten and a half miles) and the other to Wellow. (A planned extension from Wellow to Radstock was never built; a link was eventually forged with a railway). It was started in 1794 and opened fully in 1805.

The key problem in building the canal was the steep climb to Midford and Combe Hay. The original answer was a special lift called the Caisson Lock, a test rig of which was built at Combe Hay. The structure consisted of a massive watertight tank, large enough to hold a narrowboat carrying thirty tonnes. The boat was firstly driven into a sort of cylindrical 'coffin' which was then sealed and immersed in the water in the watertight tank. The coffin was then lowered (or raised) through the tank to the next level, when the end was opened and the boat allowed to float out. The time taken to raise or lower a narrowboat over the seventy feet of the test rig was just minutes - considerably faster than could be achieved using a system of conventional locks. However, the problems of maintaining a watertight system with late eighteenth century technology were simply too great. The company reverted to the conventional and built a flight of twenty-two locks to take boats down to the K&A junction.

After a number of highly profitable years, the usefulness of the SCC came to an end when the railways reached the collieries in the 1870s. The

Dundas Wharf

company went into liquidation in 1893. Shortly thereafter the canal was derelict and was closed at the turn of the century. Interestingly, GWR used the route to build the Limpley Stoke to Camerton line. Means nothing? Well, the line shot to fame (if not fortune) when it was used as the location of the film 'The Titchfield Thunderbolt'. Freshford was used for the village scenes. Sadly, (and despite the happy ending of the film), it too closed in 1951.

When you look down at the SCC from the footbridge, you can get a clear view of the difference between a narrow canal and the K&A. Whereas the 'broad' K&A can take barges as wide as fourteen feet, the narrow canals (and most English Midland canals were narrow) usually only took boats as wide as seven feet.

This half section of the walk ends here at Dundas Wharf.

All that's left of Dundas Wharf is the splendid crane and two stone buildings; the left-hand one is a toll-house ,the other a small warehouse.

The roadway to the left of the toll-house passes up to the A36. At the top is a small lay-by. The A36 is served by a very regular bus service to Bath or Bradford. There is a stop near the lay-by. Go up to the road and turn left for the Viaduct Hotel public house (quarter of a mile).

B. DUNDAS AQUEDUCT to BATH

Distance:	5¹/₂ miles/9 kilometres
Map:	OS Landranger 172 (Bristol, Bath & surrounding area)
Transport:	BR: Bath-Bradford but no stop on this section. Enquiries to 0225-463075
	Bus: Badgerline 264 & 265 (Bath-Bradford buses) stop at Dundas Aqueduct and Bathampton (ask driver for best stop). Enquiries to 0225-464446
Car Parks:	Dundas: Lay-by on A36
	Claverton: Lay-by on A36; on-road on minor road that runs down to the pumping station
	Bathampton: Near George Inn
	Sydney Gardens: On-road near gardens
	Bath: Several car parks in town
Tourist Info:	Bath on 0225-462831

If you're joining the route from the A36 lay-by or bus stop, pass down the minor road that runs east opposite the turning to Monkton Combe. If at the Viaduct Inn, walk back in the direction of Bath and take the first right turn.

When you reach the canal, take the advice offered by the towpath sign and turn left. Pass the wharf crane and take the path to the left of the old stone warehouse. This goes around the back of the building and up to Dundas Bridge (note stop gates). Cross the bridge and turn left to continue the walk along the good, firm path on the right-hand (east-facing) bank of the canal.

The route continues with fine views down right to the River Avon and the railway. Within half a mile, you will pass Millbrook Swing Bridge. Turn left here for the A36 and a small area of car parking. The towpath continues on the right bank.

Within a short distance on the right-hand side, nearly buried in the hedge, is a most curious roller-like object. This was once attached to a chain with a plug. By closing the surrounding stop gates (or using the stop planks), a temporary mini-pound could be isolated. The plug could then be pulled using the crank system that you can see rusting just here (the water drained to the Avon) and the clay puddling checked and repaired if necessary.

Walk on to Claverton Road Bridge. On the right is a small lane

Claverton pumping station

(Ferry Lane) which leads down to a railway crossing and then to a bridge. On the left is a mill pond and Claverton Pumping Station.

The Claverton Pumping Station is a true wonder. It was completed in March 1813 and was designed to improve the water supply at this end of the canal. Although the Somerset Coal Canal, the Wilts and Berks Canal and the Seend feeder all added water to the K&A, there was still a shortage. So, after lengthy negotiations, the Claverton grist mill and water rights were bought from the Duke of Somerset and a pumping house was built. And what a pump! The system is composed of a large water-wheel (eighteen feet in diameter and twenty-five feet wide) which uses the River Avon as its driving force. The water-wheel then powers two beams and pumps. The pumping force is terrific; water being lifted from the River Avon to the canal forty-seven feet up the hill at the rate of 100,000 gallons an hour.

The pump originally worked twenty-four hours a day (assuming no breakdowns, of which there were a few). But, as the canal grew more and more derelict, so it was worked less and less. In 1952 it stopped altogether - a log got through the simple filtering system and caused a jam which resulted in some of the wooden teeth on the pit wheel (ie. not the water-wheel itself but one of the power transfer wheels) shearing off. The pump came to a grinding halt and was quickly replaced by diesel power. Everything was then left to fall apart until the cavalry (in the shape of the K&A Canal Trust) came over the hill and saved the day. With the help of the engineering department of the nearby Bath University, it has lovingly restored the pumps to health. Like Crofton, the pumping house is open and working on weekends throughout the summer (check with the Devizes Canal Centre 0380-721279). However, nowadays, water is raised to the canal by means of electric pumps, most of the time.

Even if it's not a weekend, you can still look at the outside of the building. But cross the railway with care! The trains do sound their horn at this point but the Bath side of the line curves away quite quickly and on-coming trains are hard to see. If the outside of the building tempts you, the trust produces a well-written, detailed and reasonably-priced booklet describing the history, engineering and reconstruction of the pump. This can be bought at the trust's shops.

Return to Claverton Road Bridge and turn right to continue along the towpath on the right-hand bank. In a short distance the delivery leat from the pumping station can be seen pouring water into the canal.

The 'castle' on the hill right is Warleigh Manor, now a school. If you continue along Ferry Lane and up to the A36 you reach Claverton village. Here in the churchyard is the mausoleum of Ralph Allen whose entrepreneurial effects we shall see when we hit Bath.

The gravel path now passes a high hedge on the right and trees on the left. We pass under Harding's Bridge. Here a sign warns us that this is Bathampton AA territory. The canal is very close to the A36 and we pass a tunnel which goes under the road on our left.

A tramway, coming down from quarries on Bathampton Down, used to pass through the road tunnel and on to Hampton Quarry Wharf.

High on the hill (Bathford Hill) on the right, is the chimney - like Brown's Folly. Built by a Mr Wade Brown for no particular reason, it has no particular architectural interest either; being just a rather dull, square tower. Perhaps the most interesting thing about it is the comment made by Headley and Meulenkamp in the excellent National Trust guide to follies. After describing the tower, they then go on to describe the local villagers at Monkton Farleigh (a mile or so north east) as '10 pence to the shilling and menacing to boot'. A comment which obviously hides an interesting adventure for the two intrepid folly hunters.

The folly is actually situated within the Avon Wildlife Trust's Brown's Folly nature reserve. The limestone grassland offers some typical plant species and, apparently, the odd green hairstreak butterfly. The hill has been designated SSSI for its oolite limestone formations and some of the old quarry caves are homes to great horseshoe bats. Those wanting more details or wishing to join the Avon Wildlife Trust should write to AWT, The Old Police Station, 32 Jacob's Wells Road, Bristol BS8 1DR.

By the way, the village and church seen at the bottom of the hill on the right is Bathford.

At this point the canal banks were becoming increasingly overgrown with weed. But presumably it is much better now than it was in 1947. In August of that year, the weed was so thick that it took a boat three days to travel from Bath to Bradford, two of which were needed for this Bath to Claverton stretch alone. Nowadays a boat can easily get from Bath to Bradford in a short afternoon. As if to prove it, on a bright autumnal Tuesday, the canal was swarming with boats of all sizes with crews of equally diverse proportions. Easily the busiest section seen so far.

After half a mile, the towpath reaches Hampton Wharf and Bathampton Swing Bridge (note route of tramway entering the wharf from the south on the western [left-hand] bank). The canal now does a quick double bend before settling itself into a south-westerly direction towards Bath. There is a factory to the right, thinly veiled by tall poplar trees, and the playing fields of King Edward's School to the left.

After passing Canal Farmhouse, the towpath passes through a gate and alongside some school buildings (Bathampton Primary) on the right. Here also is Saint Nicholas' Church (not a gudgeon to be seen). A towpath sign proffers Bath (town centre about two miles distant). The towpath passes under the bridge and out to a small green with a seat. Here on the right is the George Inn.

The canal must have come as a bit of a shock to the George. Its front door originally opened where the canal now stands, so the entrance had to be moved around the corner to its present location. The pub also sits uneasily several feet below the level of the canal. From the bridge it gives the impression of having sunk. The building is said to go back to the fourteenth century being originally associated with the priory at Bathampton.

There is room for on-road parking here. By turning right and passing the George Inn, the road eventually crosses the Avon by means of a toll bridge and then goes up to the A4 at Batheaston.

Just after the George, there is a row of terraced houses (Canal Terrace) on the right and a series of new houses on the left.

The new houses on the left have replaced the former Plasticine factory that is pictured in some books. The factory was owned by the man who invented the stuff no less. For those involved in trivia quizzes, his name was William Harbutt.

In case you're wondering, the Avon is now a good half mile north of here. At one time the company must have considered using the Avon for navigation as far as Bradford (or a least as far as Bathampton/Batheaston) rather than building a totally new watercourse. It would certainly have saved considerably on the cost of building the aqueducts, as well as avoiding the immense problems with subsidence and leakage. It is suggested that the original committee decided not to do this because of the cost of compensating the mill owners and the problems involved in re-establishing the mills in exactly the same form as they were before the canal was built. One could certainly foresee endless rows and claims of compensation on a river that would be substantially altered to make it navigable. It is perhaps also worth noting that the subsidence and leakage problems were probably unknown to them at the time the decision was made. With the additional problems of water level variation in a river navigation, the decision was heavily sided and the present route was settled on.

The stretch from Bathampton to the outskirts of Bath at Darlington Wharf is a good one and a quarter miles and roughly straight. There are two bridges along the section. The first is Candy's Bridge and the second Folly's Footbridge (with stop gates). Both lead to houses that run on either side of the A36.

The view to the right all the way along tells us that we are entering the city of Bath. Beyond Bathampton meadows are the backs of the line of houses alongside the A4. Beyond that and further forward are the remarkably steeply stacked houses that bristle up Lansdown Hill towards the racecourse. The bald, houseless hill to the right is Little Solsbury Hill, the site of somewhat older housing, viz an Iron Age hill fort. The railway stays close to the canal all along the way and the Avon gradually gets closer as we approach Bath itself.

The view left is mostly of trees and parkland that runs up to the houses (they must have a spectacular view) on the A36 Warminster road.

At the end of the straight section, the canal takes a sudden diversion left. A wall now lines the right-hand, towpath side. Just over the wall is the railway and beyond that derelict housing.

It must have been severely irritating to the K&A Company that its arch rivals, the GWR, got permission to divert the canal at this point. The narrow gap through which both had to pass certainly made it necessary but no less galling. If you look over the edge of the wall, you can still make out where the canal would once have gone and how the railway cuts it up in true motorway fashion. Basically the whole canal was shifted left a bit to make room for the rail cutting. This all happened in 1839 and caused the canal to be closed for a total 383 hours. The GWR paid £7,660 in compensation but, of course, eventually the canal company went out of business and GWR owned the whole thing.

About three-quarters of the way round the bend on the left-hand side was Darlington Wharf. From here in the 1830s passengers could catch the 'Scotch' boat (a wrought iron vessel called the Swallow that was brought from Scotland) which would take them to Bradford-on-Avon. In 1837 there were two trips a day and the forty or so passengers would take the one and a half hour journey accompanied by a 'string band' which entertained them. With tea and scones and a good strawberry jam, it must have been jolly pleasant.

The canal now passes into the short (eighty-five yard) Sydney Gardens Tunnel which passes under Beckford Road (A36) and into Sydney Gardens.

At the time the canal was built, Sydney Gardens was privately owned and definitely up-market. The proprietors of the gardens demanded both 2,000 guineas and some 'beautication' for the right to take the canal through their property. As part of that beautification, the canal was hidden at both ends by means of tunnels and the section in between has two most ornate wrought-iron bridges, both of which were made at George Stothert's

'New' railway cut, Bath

foundry in Coalbrookdale in 1800.

The second tunnel is particularly interesting because on top of it is Cleveland House, a fine example of Georgian Bath, and which (after being originally built for the Duke of Cleveland) became the headquarters of the K&A Canal Company. You get a splendid view of the place from the iron bridges. It has, I'm afraid to say, descended to being a Department of the Environment office, but still manages an air of dignity. As you pass through its tunnel, keep a look out for a shaft which passes up and into the building. I'm assured that messages (either verbal or written) were passed from the K&A office to passing boats via this rather elaborate mechanism. How the office clerk, deep in the bowels of the building, knew that a particular boat was passing and how he timed the drop isn't clear - but it makes a good story.

At the end of the tunnel, climb up the steps on the right and cross the canal by means of the footpath which goes along the back of Cleveland House. The path now turns right and, at the bidding of a towpath signpost, continues down a slope to reach the canal's left bank. Within a few hundred yards the path passes the formerly very busy Sydney Wharf (this was where the Somerset coal was unloaded),

Sydney Gardens and Cleveland House, Bath

goes up a cobblestone path to the side of Sydney Wharf road bridge and then to Bathwick Road. The route onwards is now invisible, so take my word that you should make for the Mercedes showroom on the right-hand side of the bridge and pass down some steps left. Turn right to continue along the towpath, which has now returned to the right-hand bank of the canal. Continue along the canal to a lock.

About fifty yards beyond the bridge, the view of the city to the right is a good one. Most notable amongst the buildings is the abbey which stands proud of the rest of the buildings. Bits of the abbey date back to Norman times but most of it dates from the turn of the sixteenth century. The site was established as one of ecclesiastical importance long before. King Edgar was crowned here in the former Saxon church in 953. It was a Norman bishop who moved his seat here from Wells and thereby sealed the importance of Bath as a religious centre from then on. The church to the left with the tall thin spire is the Roman Catholic Church of Saint John.

On the left-hand side, amongst the houses, is the Hugh Baird maltings,

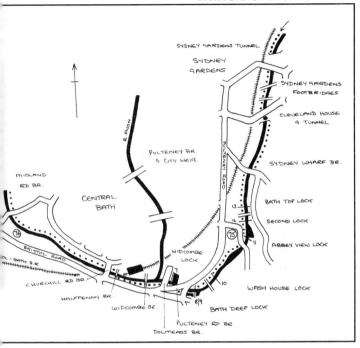

now converted to offices.

The lock is Bath Top Lock, quickly followed by one of Stothert's wrought-iron footbridges. This is the first lock since Bradford-on-Avon and the downstream end of the nine-mile pound. From here on, the canal has to make a quick, steep descent to the River Avon which is now just under half a mile away. Immediately to the right of the lock is the small lock-keeper's cottage, once taken over by the Bath Humane Society, an organisation that supplied all the lifebuoys and drag poles hereabouts.

The towpath descends quickly to Second Lock after which the canal broadens to form a reservoir pound with the same purpose as those at the Caen Hill flight in Devizes. The path now curves round right, passing a solitary chimney on the other side of the hedge, to reach Abbey View Lock and Horseshoe Walk Bridge which carries the comparatively quiet Horseshoe Walk Road.

155

Two pumping stations were built on this descent to the Avon with a view to providing a much needed alternative water supply to the nine-mile pound. Every time a boat passed through Bottom Lock, a lockful of water was lost downstream to the Avon. In periods of heavy use the canal simply ran short of water. To resolve the problem, one pumping station was built at the bottom of the Widcome flight, the other was put here just above Abbey View Lock. The intention was that the lower engine would pump water to the pound adjacent to the upper engine, from whence it would then be further raised to the pound above Top Lock. At one point, the canal company pumped water from the Bottom Lock chamber with the gate opened, effectively removing Avon water. This was declared illegal and the Avon mill owners had the pumping stopped. As a result the engines were taken out in 1855. All that's left of the upper station is the ornamental chimney that can be seen on the city side of the canal at this point; a kind of industrial folly.

Cross Horseshoe Walk and pass down the towpath. There are some steep sloping allotments on the left. Wash House Lock is immediately followed by another fine wrought-iron footbridge. Just before the church the canal curves right to Bath Deep Lock.

After a road improvement scheme, it was found necessary to amalgamate Chapel and Bridge Lock to form Bath Deep Lock (now designated number 8/9). And it is deep! In fact, it's the deepest lock in the entire British canal system at 18ft 8ins (5.69m). Because of the amount of water required, a pump was installed to move water back upstream after use.

To avoid having to cross the busy Pulteney Road Bridge, pass over the canal at the downstream lock gate. From there, take the steps which pass down right to a concrete path which goes under the road (take the opportunity to look back at the massive lock gates covered in all manner of vegetative growth). The path continues under a second road bridge (Baptist Chapel Bridge which carries Rossiter Road) and out to Thimble Mill Basin an expanded area of water. Here on the other side of the 'lagoon' is the recently built Bath Hotel.

There is now just a few yards of the 1810 K&A Canal left. The path passes the final lock, Bottom or Widcome Lock, which sits next to Thimble Mill. Pass over Dolmeads Bridge and take the lower metalled pathway that goes down to the River Avon which, massive by comparison, suddenly bursts on the scene from the right.

The K&A joins the Avon at Widcombe Flight, Bath

Thimble Mill was the lower of the two pump houses that were discussed earlier. It now houses a restaurant.

This final flight of locks - the Widcome flight - took a lot of completing. Although started fairly early on in the building programme, the first boat (carrying forty tons of stone) passed up the canal from the River Avon on 10th November 1810. Although the general public had apparently lost their enthusiasm after such a long wait, the guns in Sydney Gardens were fired in celebration of the event. Sadly, nothing so exciting happened when I reached this point although somehow I felt it should have done.

Progress from here depends on where you're going. If you wish to carry on immediately, continue along the metalled towpath by the side of the Avon and under the green footbridge in front of you. If you want to visit the town centre via Pulteney Bridge (well worth a visit) go back up to Dolemeads Bridge, turn left and walk along the Avon path until you reach the bridge (about half a mile). The railway and bus stations can be more speedily reached by returning to Dolemeads Bridge and taking the higher of the two paths alongside the Avon. Within 100 yards, you will reach the green footbridge (Widcombe Bridge - more about which is included in the next section). After crossing the bridge, continue straight and pass through a short tunnel. Turn left at the end for the BR station. The bus station is about seventy-five yards from the railway station towards the town centre.

Bath is a big place and well stocked with shops, eating/drinking places and accommodation at all prices. It is also, of course, well stocked with history and interest.

It's said that it was a spa town even before the Romans came but it was they that made the town of Aquae Sulis into something special. Anyone visiting Bath MUST visit the Roman Baths (despite the relatively high price), so much of which has only recently been discovered. It seems surprising that the baths disappeared so quickly after the Romans left in the fourth century, the whole area apparently becoming immersed under a thick layer of mud and not seen again until the nineteenth century. Despite this, from the seventeenth century, Bath was renowned as a bathing and healing centre, and by the eighteenth century the place was crawling with an early form of yuppie who used the city as a kind of West Country Saint Tropez.

It was at this time that Bath expanded dramatically. Richard (Beau) Nash came to the fore as the uncrowned King of Bath. With his political push, with the enterprise of the entrepreneur, Ralph Allen, and with the design work of the John Woods (Junior and Senior - both architects), Bath was made into the city we see today. The Woods were responsible for some of the most famous sites; the Royal Crescent, the Circus and the Assembly Rooms as well as Allen's house at Prior Park. With all this activity, it is of no coincidence that one of the key proprietors of the Avon Navigation was Ralph Allen, and that he was one of the first and most successful users of it. The navigation allowed Allen to open up the Bathampton and Combe Down quarries both for local use and for trade along the now usable river. His quarries were connected via a tramway to a wharf at Widcombe.

Pulteney Bridge, incidentally, is somewhat later than the Nash-Allen-Wood period, being built in 1770 for Sir William Pulteney to a design by Robert Adam. By 1820 Bath as we see it was virtually complete. Almost all new development within the town centre results from war time bomb damage.

It is now your chance to wallow in tourism and Bath buns for the rest of the afternoon.

❋   ❋   ❋

8. THE K&A WALK
BATH to BRISTOL

It's hard for this last part of the K&A Walk to live up to the heights of the Bradford-Bath section but we now enter the fascinating and highly rewarding final stretch. Mind you, it does have its problems; there are some parts that wouldn't rate high on any scale of beauty. Other portions, meanwhile, offer superb and relaxing scenery. At Bristol we meet a city head on; its uncomprising lows and its absorbing highs. Whatever this section has or does not have, it certainly has extreme variety.

After the cosiness of the canal, we are back to a walk along a mature and meandering river. The K&A proper has finished and we are now making our way along John Hore's Avon Navigation of 1727. At first the sheer width of the river takes some getting used to; the other bank seems so far away. Eventually the similarity between the Avon and parts of the Thames makes the surroundings more familiar and somehow more friendly. Unfortunately, .partly through lack of access and partly because the navigation is passing through urban areas, some lengths of the walk are alongside busy roads. If you wish to avoid this, it may be advisable firstly to take the railway path (see text) and secondly to stop your walk at Conham (three and a half miles short of Bristol floating harbour). From there you can take public transport into the centre of the city. But having got this far...

Although there are ample transport connections between Bristol and Bath, the number of times that either train or bus contact the river en route is relatively small. In practice only Saltford, Swineford and Keynsham offer true, easy return points along the way. But be ready to be impressed. The what could be eight hour walk from Bath to Bristol is covered by an Inter-City 125 in just eight minutes!

You'll almost certainly buy something in Bath (how can you resist) but Saltford and Keynsham, plus some parts of the Bristol suburbs, can be used for supplies if necessary. Pubs are once again numerous all along the way.

A. BATH to KEYNSHAM

Distance:	9 miles/15 kilometres
Map:	OS Landranger 172 (Bristol, Bath & surrounding area)
Transport:	BR: Bristol-Keynsham-Bath. Enquiries to 0225-463075 Bus: Badgerline X3, X4, 336, 337 & 339 from Bristol stop at Keynsham (not X3/4) and Saltford on their way to Bath. At Swineford Badgerline 331, 332 & 632 and Andrews Coaches 452 also wend their way back to Bath. Enquiries to 0225-464446
Car Parks:	Bath: Several signposted car parks in town New Bridge (on A4): Park and ride on city side of river Saltford: On-road near High Street Swineford: On-road near the Swan pub Keynsham: Signposted in town
Tourist Info:	Bath on 0225-462831

The walk starts at the Thimble Mill at the end of the K&A Canal's Widcome Locks. To reach this point from the bus and railway station, go through the tunnel to the left of the railway station entrance. Carry straight on and over the green Widcombe Footbridge. Turn left after a redundant toll-house at the end of the bridge, and walk for about 100 yards towards the well-labelled Thimble Mill. Do not cross Dolmeads Bridge but turn 180° left and pass down the metalled path to the river. An Avon Walkway signpost indicates Churchill Bridge. The path passes down and under the footbridge.

On 6th June 1877 the Bath & West Agricultural Show was held at Beechen Cliff, Bath, and it attracted thousands of people many of whom came by train. The quickest way to the showground from the station was by way of the Widcombe (then called the Ha'penny) Footbridge which at that time was a toll bridge. Following the arrival of a particularly crowded train, the bridge was soon full of people waiting to pay their toll. Suddenly the floor of the bridge crumpled and the tie-rods and girders fell away from the masonry. People were literally poured into the river below, thrown onto the towpath or buried under debris. Nine or ten people were killed and forty to fifty seriously injured. Aren't you glad I told you AFTER you'd crossed?

As you pass under the bridge, have a look at the stone work on the left. Various official graffiti artists have inscribed the flood heights over the

Canal near Cadley Lock

Wharf at Devizes

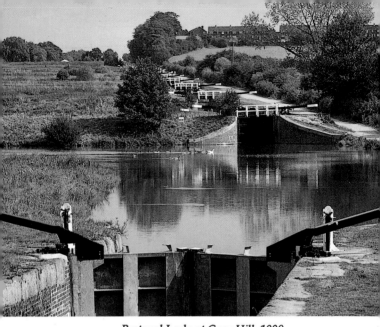

Restored Locks at Caen Hill, 1990

Avoncliff Aqueduct

years. The highest I could see was 15th November 1894. Any higher bids?

The Avon Walkway is a route all along the River Avon towpath ending at Pill near Avonmouth. The signposting is a bit sporadic in places compared with the excellently posted K&A path so don't rely on it.

The path continues under the railway bridge (Bath-Bristol line) and then up to a new Halfpenny or Southgate Footbridge. Cross the bridge to the right-hand (northern) bank and turn left. (Continue straight on for the Southgate shopping area).

The railway bridge was originally constructed of wood and you can't help thinking that it must have been more pleasant than this one. Southgate Footbridge was opened in 1964. There has been some degree of bridge shuffling just here. A former bridge - Saint Lawrence's - was demolished in the same year and was replaced by the dual carriageway Churchill Bridge (opened October 1965).

While we're on bridges, Brunel's splendid castellated railway bridge to the left is worth taking a second look at. It bears a remarkable resemblance to his design for Temple Meads station in Bristol.

Cross the road at Churchill Bridge (easier said than done) and continue along the right-hand bank of the river. Fifty yards after the bridge, a combined Avon Walkway/Bristol & Bath Railway Path sign points us in the right direction. Take advantage of the seat here to catch your breath, after all that road crossing, and admire Bath's own docklands development of warehouse conversions on the southern bank.

The part of the Avon from here right through to Bristol and the sea was always navigable. Bath received supplies of wine, wax, salt, wool, skins and cloth by river. At least that was until the Middle Ages when, like many of the country's rivers, the way became obstructed by mill owners positioning weirs along their stretch in order to produce a better head of water.

There were various attempts during the seventeenth century to make the Avon navigable to Bath but none succeeded. In 1699 Bath Corporation wanted to make the Avon navigable but was defeated by the combined powers of the gentry, farmers and traders who feared ruin through the competition from cheaper goods imported by water transport.

By the eighteenth century, things were very different. As described, Ralph Allen and other entrepreneurs (like John Hobbs, a Bristol deal merchant, and the Duke of Beaufort) saw the opportunities for business, particularly with the development of Bath at that time. Although there was

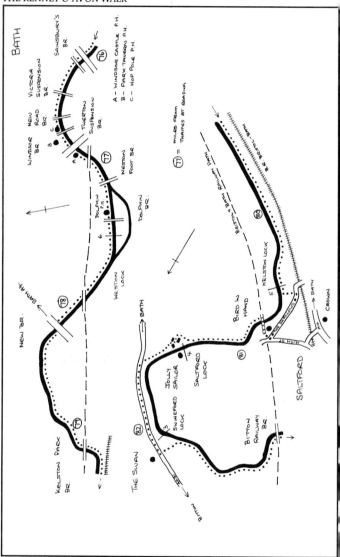

A - WINDSOR CASTLE P.H.
B - PARK TAVERN P.H.
C - HOP POLE P.H.

(77) = MILES FROM THAMES AT READING

some delay after the parliamentary act was passed in 1712, once the entrepreneurs had power, work started immediately. In 1724 John Hore of Newbury was employed to manage the works. By December 1727 the navigation (including six locks) was fully opened to traffic from Hanham to the Bath city weir (remember that Pulteney Bridge didn't come until later). The tidal Avon, from Hanham to the sea, remains under the control of the Port of Bristol Authority. Interestingly there was no towpath, the barges were hauled by men. Knowing this fact, it might come as a surprise that passenger boats started to go from Bristol to Bath in 1730. The journey took a speedy four hours and cost a shilling. Would you pull a boat from Bristol to Bath for that?

The path deteriorates somewhat and alder trees grow along the bank. On the far side old warehouses are being converted. Pass under Midland Road Bridge (an iron bridge that was being very noisily grit blasted as I went underneath). Here on the right is Sainsbury's and the next bridge is called Sainsbury's Bridge. The path has now turned into a dirt track and proceeds through some high shrubs. After a mixture of new and old warehousing, and some typical Bath houses (Norfolk Crescent), the path goes under a fine, green suspension bridge (the Victoria Suspension Bridge built in 1836) and another iron bridge (New Road Bridge). The gas works is now on the left.

The gas works made good use of the K&A canal system. Coal was shipped down the Somerset Coal Canal to Dundas, through Bath and along the Avon to here.

The river now bends left to pass under a bridge carrying a gas pipe and a road bridge (Twerton Suspension Bridge). Here on the right is the Windsor Castle pub. After some new houses, we take our first turn under the redundant Midland Railway Mangotsfield-Bath line.

If you're reading this rather than walking it, you may have already realised that this is not the scenic, touristy part of Bath. Indeed, I shouldn't think an American coach party has ever gone this way. And who can blame them really? It's a mixture of grimy industrial buildings, derelict warehouses and new 'instant' commercial units, and there's still just over a mile of it to go.

The Midland Railway's Mangotsfield line terminated at Bath's fine Green Park station, a much more handsome building than Brunel's Bath

Spa station, and now reduced to a car park. The line opened in 1869 and closed in 1966. The station, however, has been partly preserved. True railway buffs will, of course, also know that Green Park was the terminus for the Somerset & Dorset Railway's line to Evercreech Junction; twenty-six miles of wonderful railway opened in 1874 and again closed in 1966. Despite the World Cup, it must have been an awful year.

The view right turns first residential and then to industrial units, newer ones this time. One of them has a series of picnic seats situated under some neatly cropped weeping willows. This building and the one across the river are part of the former Bath Cabinet Makers Company, now Arkana Ltd. Pass under the rickety footbridge.

At Twerton the river splits. The main stream continues onwards to a weir. The towpath follows the Western Cut right.

There was formerly a ferry at this point taking people from one side of the river to the other. The island formed from the digging of the cut is called Dutch Island. Supposedly this is because of the former mill owner who lived there, who was, you've guessed it, Dutch.

After passing a small humpback bridge that reminds one of the K&A (Dolphin Bridge dated 1728 and partially rebuilt after a bomb landed on one side during the Second World War), the Dolphin Inn is on the right. Just after is a road with a bus stop and some car parking spaces. Within a short distance, we reach the end of the cutting. Here is Weston Lock.

Being a lock attendant might seem to be a fairly pleasant, if poorly paid, occupation. However, it wasn't all a bed of roses. Here at Weston Lock, Thomas Hawkins was lockman when the canal opened for the princely salary of £20 a year. Was it worth it? Lock keepers not only had to see boats through the lock but had to check that the correct toll had been paid for the cargo on board: easy if the bargeman was honest, harder if he wasn't. Bargemen would commonly understate the cargo weight in order to get away with a lower fee. Sometimes this resulted in violence as in 1728 when John Price of Bath was refused passage through the lock until he had paid the correct amount. In the ensuing fracas, Price broke open the lock gates by force and passed through. A similar thing happened when one barge owner demanded passage after 7pm, knowing that night-time use of locks was declared illegal by the company.

As you pass back down to the river, look back up the course of the main stream to see the massive weir. Relief is arriving for town-walk haters on the right side at least: Twerton Wood now masks the busy A36 and Bristol-Bath railway. On the right, there is still a number of houses and factories to come. About half a mile after Weston Lock, we pass under another Midland Railway bridge.

Here walkers could go up to the Bristol-Bath Railway Path; a metalled cycle route which goes from here to near Willsbridge. It makes good walking (although you have to occasionally dodge out of the way of speeding bikes) and those in a hurry could take this path as far as Bitton (just before Keynsham). This action could save about one-and-a-half to two miles walking (including three-quarters of a mile of not particularly pleasant road near Swineford), and, because it is so much easier underfoot, could save three-quarters of an hour at least. If you do take it, you have to return to the towpath at the third crossing of the river.

Towpath huggers will now get the relief they've been seeking as the industrial area of Bath comes to an end. On the right, a new marina is being built and on the left there are open fields. Shortly we reach a wooden footbridge that passes over the entrance to the marina and then to the handsome New Bridge.

New Bridge, or Weston Bridge, is made of Bath stone and has a splendid 100 foot span bracketed by a series of flood arches. The large circular holes that pass through the main body of the arch are attractive and presumably deliberate but appear to have no real purpose.

The road here is the A4. Turn right to go back to Bath or left for a road route to Saltford. On the right is a huge car park that forms part of the Bath park and ride scheme. Some, but not all, of the Keynsham-Bath buses pass along this road.

The path goes through one of the flood arches and turns right to go up to the road. Pass over the bridge (passing a marker indicating the city limits) and then down the steps on the far side to the towpath, which now takes the left-hand (southern) bank. Here a concrete path winds its way to a small building. Bear right and pass over the stile to go down a track, squeezed between the building and the river. This ends with another stile which takes us into the open field and along a muddy grass track.

The river and the walker are now much more relaxed. With open fields on the left and a tree-covered hillside to the right, the scenery becomes reminiscent of the Thames.

The river gradually curves left and passes under the Midland Railway.

High on the hill on the right is Kelston Park house, yet another designed by John Wood Jnr.

Just as the river bends right here (immediately before the railway embankment), the Avon navigation map marks a huge meander. Seemingly the course of the river was straightened in 1971. If it was, there appears to be no sign of a meander now.

The path bears left a fraction to pass over a small footbridge which crosses Corston Brook. For the next three-quarters of a mile, the path is wedged in an area of dense undergrowth between the railway and the river.

This area of woodland is thick with blackthorn bushes and it is clearly a popular haunt for collectors of sloes. All the little, ripe, black berries were high on the bushes and none were within easy reach - a sure sign of a well-worked area.

The woodland clears and the path crosses a stile to pass in front of some buildings: a redundant clubhouse with crazy paving up the wall and some run down boathouses. Stay right of the small fence and walk over some wooden jetties. Cross an extraordinarily tall concrete and stone footbridge. Saltford Marina is now on the left. Kelston Lock can be seen on the far bank and a new clubhouse with a 'Boater's Bar' on this bank. The path continues alongside some pollarded willow trees to a fence which pushes walkers right and out to a minor road - 'The Shallows'. Turn right along the road to pass the Saltford Brass Mill on the right.

At one time the River Avon had numerous brass works along its length. The occurrence of all these mills just here is an accident of geography. Brass is an alloy of copper and zinc and was discovered in seventeenth century to be terribly useful for making all manner of objects like pots and pans. Zinc was mined just south of here in the Mendip hills (originally in the form of calamine - zinc oxide). Copper was brought in from Cornwall and usually smelted on site. With the abundant water power, the industry prospered. Skilled workers from Holland were attracted into the area and products were shipped to places as diverse as India and the United States.

Saltford Brass Mill was formerly a fulling mill (a mill which cleaned wool using fuller's earth) and only became a brass mill in 1721. It was still going strong in 1908 as a brass battery mill and sheet rolling continued until 1925. The Avon industry, however, eventually lost out to competition from south Wales (most notably the Swansea valley) and from native mills in the main export market of the United States.

A battery mill, incidentally, used massive hammers to 'batter' the brass into shape. One oft-repeated story in these parts is that Handel wrote the Hallelujah Chorus after hearing the rhythm of the hammers here at Saltford. A story which takes a bit of beating.

The towpath has now changed banks but there is no ready way of crossing the river near the mill. As a result continue along The Shallows for about quarter of a mile. There is room for car parking here. At the Bird in Hand public house turn right into Mead Lane. Just after the pub car park take the steps to the right which pass up to the Bristol-Bath Railway Path. Turn right and walk for about fifty yards to the bridge which carries the path over the river. At the far end of the bridge bear left down a steep and slippery slope back to the river. Turn right and continue through a field along the right-hand bank.

To visit the centre of Saltford or to catch one of the Bath to Bristol buses, turn left at the Bird in Hand (along the shopless High Street) and then left again at Beech Road. After half a mile in total, you will reach the A4 Bath Road. Here you will find toilets, shops, the Crown pub and bus stops.

If you go this way, keep an eye open for the church and manor house to your right. The manor house is reputed to be the oldest inhabited building in the country, with some parts of it being built in Norman times.

The Bird in Hand, by the way, was opened in 1869 as an inn for the men of the Midland Railway. It must have had quite a rivalry with a pub further along Mead Lane, the Jolly Sailor, which was opened to serve the men working on the river navigation.

The grassy path, fringed with alder and hawthorn trees, passes alongside an open field and over two stiles. Within half a mile, the Jolly Sailor public house appears on the left-hand bank, with a lock (Saltford Lock) farther along the river and houses (the outskirts of Kelston) on this side in the near distance.

The Jolly Sailor was quite an important stopping place for bargemen as it offered hospitality for both men and horses. The fireplace in the bar was also the scene of a navigators' ritual. When a bargeman was promoted to master, he heated a poker in the fire and then drove it into the wooden surround. Whether or not he then bought everyone in the bar a drink seems to be a matter of debate.

It's slightly confusing that the Kelston Lock is in Saltford and Saltford Lock is in Kelston. I thought that it was a printing error on the navigation map but apparently it's due to some (obviously complicated) parish boundaries hereabouts.

The opening up of the river to traffic was received with as much enthusiasm by certain people in this area as the opening of the Kennet Navigation was by the people of Reading. Basically they hated the idea. For the first time the Avon Navigation made it possible to import cheap and superior quality Shropshire coal and the Somerset miners saw it as a clear danger to jobs. Numerous threats were made to destroy the navigation and things got so serious that parliament had to install the death penalty for wilful damage to the works of a navigable river. Even this didn't stop the attacks. Saltford Lock was wrecked in November 1738 and almost destroyed. A note was left saying that 'much greater mischief' would occur if the navigation kept importing Shropshire coal. Luckily there wasn't and the Somerset fields went on to prosperous times, despite the competition.

Take the path 'inland' and pass to the right of the cottages to a gate. Turn left and walk along the path in front of the houses to a small green. Here on the left is the Kelston brass (battery) mill with its two annealing ovens still standing (annealing is the process of tempering the metal by heating it). As the road bends right next to a telephone box take the track left between the two cottages and over a stile. Turn left and walk next to the wall. Cross the field (passing close to the river) to a stile in the hedge. After the stile and a small bridge that crosses a brook take a straight course across the field and over a stile to a road. Cross to the pavement on the other side of the road and turn left.

The next half to three-quarters of a mile is by the side of the relatively busy A431. This is a bit dire but, if life is getting you down, you can catch a bus here to either Bath or Bristol (nos 331, 332, 452 or 632). The other benefits include a peculiar corrugated iron church and the Swan Inn. There is also a small amount of parking near the pub.

The Swan and the 'centre' of Swineford marks the end of the road walk. Opposite the pub and just after a telephone box a footpath sign directs walkers across a muddy field in the direction of the river.

Swineford is said to derive its name from the time when a prince contracted leprosy. Because of this he took a job as pigman. Unfortunately the pigs caught the disease as well. He was naturally a bit depressed by now and drove his pigs across the mud just here. Imagine his surprise (if you can) when the pigs came out of the mud cured (in the sense of being relieved of illness rather than being made into bacon). He, naturally enough, dived in and, not to our surprise, was similarly miraculously cured. I don't actually recommend rolling around in the mud on the other side of the fence (walking through it proved to be enough of a trial) but if you're feeling a bit poorly, do you have anything to lose?

The mill to the left, as you roll across the field, ended its days as a woollen mill but was originally one of the Avon brass mills.

Our diversion via the road has meant that we've missed Swineford Lock which was on the river just opposite the church. However, we do not miss the beginning of the territory of the Bristol & West Federation of Anglers. We are about two and a half miles from Keynsham.

Turn right when you reach the river and follow the worn grass track along the bank and across a stile. To the right is the village of Bitton with its church which is apparently haunted by a lady in grey. Further round large commercial greenhouses outcrop on the hill. After a few bends the path passes under the old Midland Railway bridge. Those who took the quick, railway path route should now descend and carry on via the towpath. Shortly after the bridge, the path crosses the River Boyd (via Ferris' Horsebridge) to a large field. The river meanders back and forth around the area known as Holm Mead. Here a number of stiles have been rendered redundant following the removal of various hedges.

About a mile after the Horsebridge the river enters the outskirts of Keynsham. A former chemical works with a chapel-like edifice (dated 1881) is on the left. After passing by a bridge carrying a pipe across the river, the path joins an unmade driveway out through a gate. After the entrance to a Caravan Club site, bear left to a narrow path alongside the river. (Ignore the tempting driveway which merely continues to the road). The path now weaves its way through banks of nettles and brambles with a precipitous drop on the left. Shortly after, the path bends abruptly right and over a footbridge next to Portavon Marina to reach Bitton Road and the Lock Keeper public house.

To get to the centre of Keynsham, walk up to the main road bridge and turn left. The BR railway station is within quarter of a mile and the town centre - with plenty of shops, eating places and buses to and from Bath and Bristol - just a short distance thereafter.

Before you reach the station, a road labelled Avon Mill Lane leads to the site of yet another brass mill. Also here is the site of a water-powered logwood mill. Natural colours from tropical woods were commonly used before the discovery of aniline and other dyes. At Albert Mill logs were shredded and the wood chips crushed using a water-driven system.

Keynsham is a country town sited on the spot where the River Chew joins the Avon. The town is said to date back to Roman times with a number of villas being found round abouts. An abbey was founded here in the twelfth century only to be later 'dissolved' by Henry VIII. The town now sits, perhaps a little overlooked, between its more illustrious neighbours of Bath and Bristol but makes a very convenient half-way point for this section of the walk.

B. KEYNSHAM to BRISTOL

Distance:	8 miles/13 kilometres
Map:	OS Landranger 172 (Bristol, Bath & surrounding area)
Transport:	BR: Bristol-Keynsham-Bath. Enquiries to 0225-463075 Bus: Badgerline 336, 337 & 339 from Bristol stop at Keynsham and Saltford on their way to Bath (very regular). The 332 passes via Hanham Abbots on the A431. Enquiries to 0225-464446
Car Parks:	Keynsham: Signposted in town Hanham Mills: Next to river near pubs Conham Vale: Next to river Bristol: Signposted in the city centre
Tourist Info:	Bristol on 0272-260767

The walk starts at the Lock Keeper public house at County Bridge on the A4175 to Willsbridge. To reach this point from the centre of town go along Station Road until you reach the railway station. From there continue along the road, passing Avon Mill Lane (right), until you reach the river bridge. The Lock Keeper pub will be found on the right. Turn right down the dead-end Bitton Road. Turn right to cross a stile and go under the road bridge.

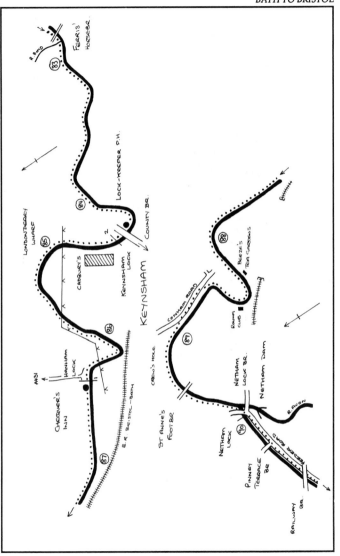

R. BOYD
FERRIS' HORSEBR.
83
LOCK-KEEPER P.H.
84
LONDON DERRY WHARF
85
CADBURY'S
KEYNSHAM LOCK
2
COUNTY BR.
KEYNSHAM
86
HANHAM LOCK
A431
CHEQUER'S INN
B.R. BRISTOL—BATH
87
CREW'S HOLE
ST ANNE'S FOOT BR.
88
BREEZE'S TEA GARDENS
CONHAM ROAD
RIVER'S CLUB
87
NETHAM LOCK BR.
NETHAM DAM
R. AVON
NETHAM LOCK
90
FEEDER ROAD
PINNEY TERRACE BR.
RAILWAY BR.
BRISTOL

Within a short distance, the path reaches Keynsham Lock, before the path bends right to pass over a stile. Here on the left is the massive structure of the Cadbury chocolate factory at Somerdale.

As you are walking on the wrong side, it's sadly not possible to nip in and request samples. I stood and sheepishly nibbled at a Kit Kat, all the time expecting some huge hand to come out and grab the offending competitor from my grasp.

Frys started making chocolate (at that time it was just drinking chocolate) in Bristol in the mid-eighteenth century. Joseph Fry was actually a pharmacist who did a bit of chocolate making on the side. This factory was built after Cadbury and Frys merged in 1918 and the Frys business was moved here from Bristol. Whilst building the foundations a Roman villa was found. It's an interesting period building and somehow strangely inoffensive for such a large piece of industry right in the middle of some otherwise pleasant countryside. Some 1,400 people are employed here producing all your favourites like Chocolate Cream, Crunchie, Double Decker, Fudge, Caramel, Picnic, Curly Wurly and, of course, Fry's Turkish Delight. If you get the whiff of the Orient as you stand and admire the factory, you might like to know that in a single eight hour shift here they make about 250,000 Turkish Delights. In my estimation, that means that in the time it's taken you to read this, about 500 of the little squidgy bars have poured off the production line.

After going over (or in one case under) a couple of stiles, the path goes over a stone bridge to reach a point where the river bends sharply left. Here cross a stile. There is a footpath sign which points right for Willsbridge and Congwell Green. This is the site of the former Londonderry Wharf.

Londonderry Wharf was one of two Avon & Gloucester Railway wharves. The other (the Avon) was opposite the 1881 chemical works on the Bath side of Keynsham. The A&G was built to provide a link between the Gloucestershire coal-field and the navigation. It is a particularly interesting railway because the K&A Canal Company subscribed to its building and it was a majority shareholder. The line went from Rodway Hill, just north of Kingswood, down to the Avon at these two wharves. The five and a half mile-long, horse-worked line was fully opened in July 1832. Initially it was a great success but traffic quickly declined so that by 1850 it was obvious that it wouldn't pay its way. The loss of custom was almost certainly due to coal owners preferring the steam-powered Midland Railway that took their product straight into Bristol. The rails were eventually lifted in 1906.

The path continues over a portion of repaired bank side and under some power lines. There is now thick woodland to the right and a view of the Cadbury plant (with its playing fields) to the left. For a while the towpath becomes embroiled in cables and pylons before they go right and we go straight on to pass around a huge loop of river. Short-cutters will have twigged this early on and gone with the cables. Both routes will end up at a stile and footpath which leads directly to Hanham Mills (the cables end up high on the hill to the left). Here on the right-hand side, next to a large car park, are two pubs to choose from: The Chequers Inn and The Old Lock & Weir.

Hanham Lock is the last, or the first, lock on the Kennet & Avon Canal. From here on the Avon is tidal and comes under the jurisdiction of the Port of Bristol Authority; a total of fourteen miles from here to the sea at Avonmouth. Hanham was the limit to navigation from Bristol up until the time of the Avon Navigation in 1727.

At one time it was possible that Hanham would be by-passed. The Bath & Bristol Canal was suggested in November 1795 as an alternative to the Avon Navigation. It was said that the Avon frequently flooded in winter, had shoals in summer and was too long. The new canal would have been on one level all the way from Bathampton to Totterdown near Bristol Temple Meads Station.

In the end an alliance of landowners and others halted the bill's passage through parliament. However, in 1809 John Rennie revived the idea with another one level route from Bath via Twerton, Saltford, Hanham and Barton Hill to a terminus at Old Market Street (near Castle Street) in the middle of Bristol - a total of thirteen and a half miles (compared with about sixteen for the Avon Navigation). A branch to the floating harbour would have added a further one and a half miles. Building this route would have needed cuttings along steep hillsides and through hills, as well as the building of an aqueduct above Keynsham.

Although the Bath & Bristol Canal Company was formed, no digging ever started. In 1812 a towpath was made on the Avon and, in 1817, the river was deepened. These actions removed two of the biggest problems with the navigation and effectively killed the idea of a Bath-Bristol canal for good. The company was later bought out by the K&A for a modest sum.

If you want to stop here, turn right alongside the Chequers and up Ferry Lane to reach Hanham Abbots and the A431 where the Badgerline

332 goes to either Bristol or Bath, roughly hourly.

Meanwhile our route passes in front of the pubs and houses with the weir to the left. Continue along an unmade road. At a junction bear left and along the dirt track.

After the minor excitement of Hanham, the river now settles into quiet country along a mini-gorge. The valley is deeply wooded and quiet. Only a sporadic train, running along the BR Bristol to Bath line on the southern side of the river, disturbs the solitude. In many ways it's the lull before the storm - so enjoy the next two miles.

We pass a footpath sign directing customers to the Elm Tree public house (at least half a mile up the hill). After two rows of neat cottages and a large house on the right, the path splits and we stay close to the river.

The deep chasm here is fascinating. It's dank and eerie with huge trees overhanging the river. When I passed, the whimpering of a dog from one of the houses echoed around like a solemn, tolling bell. The rock here is a red sandstone (used quite a lot in Bristol's buildings) and periodically one can see areas where it has been quarried out of the 150-foot-high hillside.

We pass a footpath sign directing people to Hanham Common and then a stand of very geometrically-spaced poplar trees. The railway has now disappeared into a tunnel and so the silence is complete. Eventually the scenery opens out somewhat and there is a footpath sign to Hanham Common Road.

If you wish to avoid the last highly industrialised section of the walk, you could sneak up this path to the A431 and catch the bus either into town or back to Bath (eg. Badgerline 332). We won't tell.

The path broadens as the river bends left. Here a big green pipe meets the path, pops in and out of the rock and disappears again, leaving us none the wiser. As we pass a house on the left, a helpful sign points to Bristol straight on and Bath back the way we have come.

Beese's Tea Garden on the opposite bank has been there a surprisingly long time. Niaill Allsop records it as being established in 1846. At that time there was a ferry to take walkers across to it. Now all we can do is stare, with our tongues hanging out, knowing that there's still four and a half miles to go to Bristol.

The railway re-appears from the tunnel and passes over a splendid-looking viaduct (or rather a sort of half-viaduct as it clings assiduously to the rock wall). The river now bends sharply right and round 180°. On the far bank is the clubhouse of the Bristol Ariel Rowing Club and then, a little later on, a water pumping station. The bank on this side is encrusted with fishermen. Within a short distance, the river bends back left.

This is Cobham Vale. On this corner is a convenient car park and WC.

The river is so close to the road at this point that there is no room for a towpath. We are forced into the narrow, busy road and there is no pavement. Luckily it only lasts a couple of hundred yards. Just as a pavement appears, so the towpath shoots left through some white-painted metal railings. The scrappy path passes a derelict site on the right and up to some new apartments.

This is Crew's Hole and, from the mid eighteenth century, the site of a copperworks, brassworks and colliery. A copper mill was started at Conham in 1690 but the main activity was later and here. By the mid eighteenth century, there were eighty-one furnaces along the Avon with a large number at Crew's Hole. The chimney on the hill to the right (Trooper's Hill) was attached to the works and was presumably placed there to disperse the fumes as much as possible.

Crew's Hole was also the site of a tar distillery; an industry apparently established to satisfy Brunel's requirement for creosote (for all those railway sleepers). The factory was built on the site of a former pottery. The tar came originally from the Bristol gas works and the industry continued until fairly recently with the Bristol and West Tar Distillers Co. With other products like benzole and pitch, this could well have been named Carcinogen Valley.

Whatever it's called, it certainly isn't pretty and the 'luxury' housing built here must be a particularly speculative venture. The design reminded me of Portmeirion, a view I can't really explain as the surrounding scenery isn't quite the same somehow.

The river now bends left, the northern bank consisting mostly of derelict industrial units. On the southern side is a huge wharf that continues for some distance.

This is the former site of the vast St Anne's Board Mills, most of which is being demolished, or at least left to fall down. It's sad to think that this was once the site of one of the leading board makers anywhere which even developed its own high speed board-making machinery (a system called the Inverform).

After some more derelict buildings, burnt-out vans and run-down units, the path passes under St Anne's Footbridge. Some further dereliction follows before the path reaches Netham. Here the river splits. The main flow continues under Netham Lock Bridge (the Sydney Harbour look-alike) and over the weir to the tidal Avon. The right-hand fork forms the feeder canal to the floating harbour.

The site on the right before the river splits has had a difficult history. At one time this was the site of Netham Brass Mill. At that time and for some time later, there was no towpath here and passing barges found the job of traversing this short section both difficult and time consuming. Later there was an ICI factory here.

As we reach Netham Lock, we effectively leave the river and rejoin a canal. We take the course of the feeder canal so titled because it takes water from the Avon to the so-called floating harbour that now forms Bristol city docks. The floating harbour was built in 1809 in an attempt to give Bristol a non-tidal dockland. A constant head of water is maintained in the harbour and it is thus independent of tidal conditions. The construction of the deepwater harbour was very much a reaction to competition from other ports and was seen as essential if Bristol was to maintain its position as Britain's number two port after London. Ships entered the floating harbour by means of a pair of locks (Entrance and Junction Locks) after passing through the Clifton Gorge.

The waterway was designed by William Jessop, a famous canal builder in his own right. For the most part, it took the course of the River Avon. The Avon itself was diverted (at Totterdown) by means of a new cut. Building the new cut was no mean feat. It was hacked out of solid rock.

Go up to the metal bridge and cross the feeder canal by means of the footbridge. Turn right and cross both carriageways of this busy road. Netham Lock and the lock keeper's cottage are here on the right.

The gates of Netham Lock are usually held open and are only closed against floods of spring tides which pass over the weir on the main course of the Avon.

For us, the feeder road is just one long, boring slog. There's no escape, I'm afraid, and interest levels won't improve much until we hit the floating harbour wharves in about two miles time. It could be worse! Niall Allsop quotes from an 1874 edition of the Bristol Mercury *which describes the area as '...the chosen home of the manure manufacturers, bone-crushing mills, knacker yards, horseflesh-boiling factories, and works which in the manufacture of chemical products throw off nauseous gases, causing stench-laden folds of air to envelope the visitor and make him involuntarily turn to the water side to try if he can breathe more easily.' So, if you're hating it, just think yourself lucky!*

The housing estate on the right is Barton Hill. This was once the site of the Great Western Cotton Factory; a massive place that at one time employed 2,000 people. The five storey building, which was put up in the 1830s, was put down in the 1960s.

After almost exactly a mile, the canal reaches Totterdown Basin and suddenly turns right.

It was at this point that the floating harbour took over the course of the Avon and the river was pushed into the new cut.

There are two possible routes to the end of the walk at Neptune's statue in the harbour area. One route turns right here to go along Avon Street, Temple Way, Castle Street, and then down to Bristol Bridge. From there the route carries on via Welsh Back to the docks.

The main route continues straight on at the point where the feeder canal bends right. The road (Cattle Market Road) now bends right and then left to pass the massive Royal Mail sorting centre and the Cattle Market pub, and go under Temple Meads BR station.

Brunel was quite an artist with his stations and Temple Meads is no exception. The Old Station (now home to a science museum), completed in 1840, is full of turrets and battlements and gives everyone the clear impression that here is something important. The new station is also not short of interest and resembles some kind of monastery.

If you have no wish to visit the docks, you could finish the walk here and now. Turn right before the busy dual carriageway and the station can be found shortly on the right.

To complete the walk, cross this road (this may take a while) and carry straight on to Clarence Road. On the left here we meet the new cut of the River Avon. We pass the Nelson Arms on the right and a green footbridge on the left. After some blocks of flats and the Mayor's Arms, cross at the pedestrian crossing just before the roundabout, if you are not already on the left-hand side of the road. Cross the dual carriageway and pass to the left of the Plimsoll House block of flats. Go along Commercial Road, pass the Velindra pub

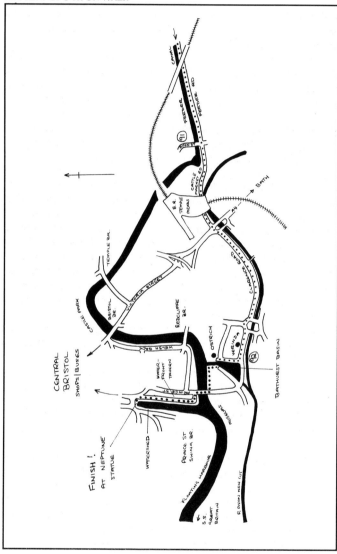

and take the first right into Lower Guinea Street. (If you have the navigation map, please note that they have labelled the streets wrongly around here).

Walk along the path with Bathurst Basin mooring on the left. At the Ostrich Inn cross the water by means of the pink swing footbridge and turn right. The end is nigh. At the end of the Wharf turn right (unless you fancy a dip) and continue until you reach a road.

On the opposite side of the road is the National Lifeboat Museum and the Bristol Industrial Museum (admission free but it is annoyingly shut on Thursdays and Fridays). Brunel's SS Great Britain is further along.

You are now standing at the heart of the floating harbour; an area of about forty hectares of dock. It is about another mile west from here to Cumberland Basin, where boats can join the tidal Avon via the two locks, and then navigate down to the open sea - a distance of about eight miles.

Although the city fathers started to worry about the issue in 1765, Jessop wasn't appointed to build the new dock until 1804. He finished it about five years later and it remains a substantial achievement. The harbour enabled large ships to moor safely without concerning themselves about fluctuating water levels. From here cargoes were unloaded onto the much smaller barges which then scuttled up and down the feeder canal to supply the industrial areas to the east of the city or even to parts of the country served by the K&A Canal.

Turn right to walk over Prince's Street Swing Bridge. At the end turn left to pass in front of the Arnolfini arts centre and then right along Narrow Quay.

Here on the right is a tourist information office-cum-YHA, and the Waterfront Tavern. On the other side is the Watershed, another arts centre. Both the Arnolfini and the Watershed have cafes.

At the very end of the quay, pass up to the street and turn left to look Neptune in the eye. You can tell him from me that you've done it.

With a population getting on for half a million, Bristol is a big, sprawling city whose growth originally depended on these docks. In fact, the city has been a commercial port since before the Norman invasion. The early trade was with Ireland and other parts of northern Europe. When the Normans arrived, the imports started to come from France (the start of Bristol's long association with wine) and from Spain.

By the Middle Ages Bristol was one of the country's major ports. From

The glass boat at 'The Floating Harbour near Bristol Bridge'

here the Brits set out to form the Empire. John Cabot set sail from Bristol to discover Newfoundland and was thus the first to actually land on the mainland of North America. On this was built Bristol's claim to be the 'Gateway to America'. Bristol became the place of import and processing of many American raw materials, perhaps most notably sugar and tobacco. Bristol also played a major part in the slave industry.

By the eighteenth century the city began to find it hard to compete with ports like Liverpool, whose docks could take much larger ships. The decline in trade was the stimulus for the building of the floating harbour. It has to be said that the floating harbour was never a huge success. Because of the high cost of building it, the mooring fees were high and by the time they realised this and reversed the pricing policy, it was too late. The city was, however, saved by the newer, and still operational, docks at Avonmouth and Portishead. There even larger ships can dock without difficulty. The floating harbour today is being developed for recreational use - everything from arts centres to museums and wine fairs to power boat races.

To reach the centre of town continue up Broad Quay to Colston Avenue and Rupert Street. The main shopping centre can then be found by turning right along Union Street. The bus station can be found a little farther along off the Haymarket. Temple Meads can be found either by retracing your steps towards the feeder canal, or by turning right along Baldwin Street, crossing Bristol Bridge and passing along Victoria Street. Here you cross a major road (passing under a flyover) to continue along Temple Street. Temple Meads station can then be found on the left.

Bristol is extremely well stocked with shops, eating and drinking places and places to stay. It's a lively place, even if you may not be after your walk.

9: THE AVON WALK
BRISTOL to the SEA

The Avon Walkway continues from the floating harbour in central Bristol, past the Entrance and Junction docks to join the tidal Avon and from there to the sea at Avonmouth. This adds an extra seven miles to the walk, producing a new total of 171 from Westminster. The Avon isn't pretty at low tide and Avonmouth isn't pretty at any tide but the Avon (Clifton) Gorge, spanned gracefully by Brunel's suspension bridge, is a magnificent sight and well worth a walk.

A. CENTRAL BRISTOL to CLIFTON SUSPENSION BRIDGE

Distance: 2¹/₂ miles / 4 kilometres

Map: OS Landranger 172 (Bristol, Bath & surrounding area)

From Neptune's statue, return to Prince's Street Swing Bridge via the Arnolfini. Turn right to pass the Bristol Industrial Museum on Prince's Wharf. This eventually became Wapping Wharf and leads to the site where the SS Great Britain is docked. The walkway now passes along Gasferry Road and out to Cumberland Road. Turn right. The Avon Walkway now joins the River Avon along a path to the left of the Cumberland Road. As the road swings right, continue alongside the river to a bridge. Cross the river to the southern (left-hand) bank. After a road bridge and a rail bridge (the latter passing over a stream), the path reaches a road. Turn right and then right again to re-cross the railway and return to the riverside.

Clifton Suspension Bridge is now in view. The idea for a bridge here started in the 1750s when one of the city's wine merchants put some money in trust for the construction of a crossing. It was largely forgotten about until 1829 when the bridge committee invited designs. Brunel tendered as he was living in Clifton at the time.

After a visit to Telford's Menai Bridge (he spent two days there in deep study apparently), he submitted a design for a suspension bridge.

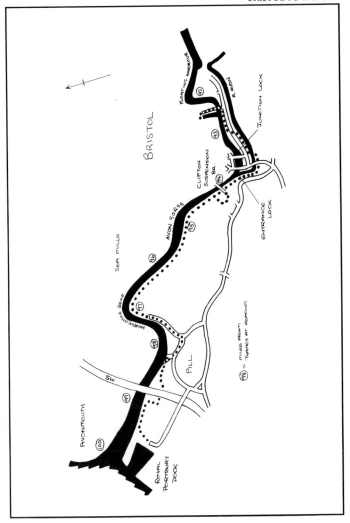

Interestingly, it was Telford who was appointed as judge for the competition and he rejected all the designs (perhaps he spotted the resemblance). He said that Brunel's was unsound because suspension bridges simply couldn't be that long. In a second competition in 1831 Brunel added a huge abutment on the Leigh Woods (left-hand) side of the gorge in order to overcome the criticisms. This design was eventually accepted and building commenced. Although the foundation stone was laid in 1836, the bridge was not completed immediately because the committee ran out of money. From 1840 until 1861 it was left unfinished. Sadly during that time Brunel died (in 1859). As a memorial to the great engineer, sufficient funds were raised and re-building started in 1861. The bridge was finally opened in 1864.

The path runs along the southern bank of the river. About 200 yards after passing under the bridge, there is an arch that passes under the railway on the left. Go through the woods and follow the path up the side of the steep-sided Nightingale Valley. Bear left at the top to reach a road. Turn left and follow the road as it bends round to meet another road. Turn left again. This will take you to the bridge. Carry straight on over the bridge to reach Clifton. Buses from here go back to the town centre.

B. CLIFTON SUSPENSION BRIDGE to PILL and the AVONMOUTH STRETCH

Distance: 5¹/₂ miles/9 kilometres

Map: OS Landranger 172 (Bristol, Bath & surrounding area)

From the point where the path leads off the towpath and into Nightingale Valley, continue walking along the towpath and through the gorge. The woods to the right are Leigh Woods. The gorge continues for about one and a half miles before flattening out.

The Bristol suburbs on the northern bank are firstly Sneyd Park and then Sea Mills. Sea Mills was formerly the site of the Roman port of Abona. Here, where the River Trym winds northwards, the first Bristol floating dock was built in the early eighteenth century. It was really a bit of a makeshift answer and Bristol eventually built the city floating dock we see today. But if you look forwards and back, you can see why Bristol docks had a problem as ships increased in size. This narrow, winding channel was

The Floating Harbour and the end of the K&A Walk

very difficult to navigate and it eventually spelt the death of the city docks in favour of Avonmouth and Portishead. Probably the most difficult section is passed next. The larger vessels could only go through Horseshoe Bend at high tide.

After a further half mile, the river turns sharply left around Horseshoe Bend below Shirehampton Park. As there is no bridge over a small stream that comes in from the left, the path goes along a small road which passes over the stream a bit farther up. This road leads to the 'townlet' of Pill. Take the next right turn along a small road past the hospital and then to a T-junction. Turn right and into the centre of the village for shops and, if you've seen enough, buses back to Bristol.

Take the road past the Swan Inn and under the railway to Union Row and then Marine Parade. After a few hundred yards the path bends away from the river only to bend back again and under the M5. Shortly thereafter the route bends back to the river. After passing under two lots of pylons, the path continues for just a short distance to Royal Portbury Dock with Avonmouth Docks on the opposite bank.

    This is the limit of pedal navigation. It might not be pretty but at least you can see the sea. You can now rest assured that you've taken the K&A Walk to its extremes. There's no round of applause or orchestra and choir. All there is to do is to chew on that chocolate biscuit that's been rattling around in the bottom of the rucksack since Westminster and to turn round and hope you can get back to Bristol before it rains. Still, well done from me.

    It is possible to continue on the path bearing left to end up on a small road which then leads back to Pill. Alternatively it is probably quicker to about face and return the way you came. In either case, Badgerline buses 340 and 341 will take you from Pill back to Bristol.

ACCOMMODATION

Providing an accommodation list is a tortuous and often thankless task, suggesting, as it does, a recommendation and some kind of responsibility for quality and value. With management changes, businesses going bust, new ones starting, prices changing, difficulties over desired price ranges etc etc, I've decided not to provide specific names and addresses but to point you in the following directions.

The Sources
Tourist information
The phone numbers of the local offices are provided in the headings for each section of the walk. Each office can suggest places to stay or camp. They should be up-to-date if occasionally a little dithery.

Rambler's Yearbook & Accommodation guide
The Ramblers' Association updates its yearbook annually (believe it or not). The accommodation list is comparatively thin but nevertheless useful. The yearbook is available in bookshops and libraries but, failing this, its address is: 1/5 Wandsworth Road, London SW8 2XX.

AA/RAC/English Tourist Board guides etc
These volumes are widely available through the relevant organisations who regularly advertise in newspapers and magazines such as the Radio Times or in bookshops (eg W.H.Smith). HOWEVER, local libraries hold the latest editions of all these guides as well as numerous others. My local library reference section has two shelves full of various guides!

The Youth Hostel Association
The YHA can provide an up-to-date list. Its address is YHA, Trevelyan House, 8 Saint Stephen's Hill, Saint Albans, Herts AL1 2DY. However, try the local library first for further information. The relevant hostels are in Bristol (on the dockside), Bath (Bathwick Hill on the way to the American Museum), Windsor (Mill Lane), and in London (nearest are in Earls Court and Victoria).

Camping

A lot of campsites never reach a list but two annuals are useful *Camping Sites in Britain* (published by Link House Magazines Ltd, Link House, Dingwall Avenue, Croydon CR9 2TA. 081-686-2599) & *Code's Camping & Touring Caravan Site Guide* (Merwain Publishing Ltd, PO Box 146, Bletchley, Milton Keynes, Bucks).

The Places

The following places are the main centres along the route. Halfway points are in brackets.

Central London (Hammersmith): Probably best to stay out of London and catch train in.

Richmond-on-Thames, London (Hampton Court, Surrey)

Weybridge, Surrey (Staines, Surrey)

Windsor, Berks (Maidenhead, Berks)

Marlow, Bucks (Henley, Oxon)

Reading, Berkshire (Theale, Berks): Not much cheap accommodation in Reading, probably best to stay outside and train/bus in.

Hungerford, Berkshire (Wilton, Wilts)

Pewsey, Wiltshire (All Cannings, Wilts): Accommodation in central Wilts could be difficult. If so, you might try Marlborough, Wilts, as an alternative, and catch the bus in.

Devizes, Wiltshire (Semington, Wilts): Note also the proximity of Trowbridge, Wilts, and Melksham, Wilts.

Bradford-on-Avon, Wiltshire (Bathampton/Monkton Combe, Wilts)

Bath, Avon (Keynsham, Avon)

Bristol, Avon

FURTHER READING

The information used in this book comes from a wide range of sources - too many to list here in its entirety. However, a small number of books could make useful sources should you wish to find out more about the walk or the canal, and are therefore heartily recommended.

The key book in all this is:
Kenneth R.Clew: *The Kennet & Avon Canal. An Illustrated History*. (2nd Ed). David & Charles, Newton Abbot.

    Mr Clew's book is essential reading for anyone interested in the navigation and its history. It's thoroughly readable and overflows with detailed information.

Other books specifically about the K&A include:
Niall Allsop: *The Kennet & Avon Canal. A User's Guide to the Waterways between Reading and Bristol*. Millstream Books.
Niall Allsop: *Images of the Kennet & Avon. 100 Years in Camera. Bristol to Bradford-on-Avon*. Redcliffe Press, Bristol.
Valerie Bowyer: *Along the Canal. The Kennet and Avon from Bath to Bradford-on-Avon*. Ashgrove Press, Bath.

Books published by the Kennet & Avon Canal Trust include:
Claverton Pumping Station
Crofton Beam Engines
A Pictorial Journey from Bath to Reading

    The standard reference books on British canals are written (or edited) by Charles Hadfield and published by David & Charles. The central volume of the series is:
Charles Hadfield: *British Canals. An Illustrated History*. David & Charles, Newton Abbot.

Other books which are of interest are:
R.A.Buchanon: *Industrial Archaeology in Britain*. Penguin Books.
Kenneth Hudson: *Industrial Archaeology of Southern England*. David & Charles, Newton Abbot.
Roger Jones: *Down the Bristol Avon*. Ex Libris Press, Bradford-on-Avon.

CICERONE GUIDES

Cicerone publish a wide range of reliable guides to walking and climbing in Britain - and other general interest books

LAKE DISTRICT - General Books
LAKELAND VILLAGES
WORDSWORTH'S DUDDON REVISITED
THE REGATTA MEN
REFLECTIONS ON THE LAKES
OUR CUMBRIA
PETTIE
THE HIGH FELLS OF LAKELAND
CONISTON COPPER A History
LAKELAND - A taste to remember (Recipes)
THE LOST RESORT?
CHRONICLES OF MILNTHORPE
LOST LANCASHIRE

LAKE DISTRICT - Guide Books
CASTLES IN CUMBRIA
WESTMORLAND HERITAGE WALK
IN SEARCH OF WESTMORLAND
CONISTON COPPER MINES
SCRAMBLES IN THE LAKE DISTRICT
MORE SCRAMBLES IN THE LAKE DISTRICT
WINTER CLIMBS IN THE LAKE DISTRICT
WALKS IN SILVERDALE/ARNSIDE
BIRDS OF MORECAMBE BAY
THE EDEN WAY

NORTHERN ENGLAND (outside the Lakes
THE YORKSHIRE DALES A walker's guide
WALKING IN THE SOUTH PENNINES
LAUGHS ALONG THE PENNINE WAY
WALKS IN THE YORKSHIRE DALES (2 VOL)
WALKS TO YORKSHIRE WATERFALLS
NORTH YORK MOORS Walks
THE CLEVELAND WAY & MISSING LINK
DOUGLAS VALLEY WAY
THE RIBBLE WAY
WALKING NORTHERN RAILWAYS EAST
WALKING NORTHERN RAILWAYS WEST
HERITAGE TRAILS IN NW ENGLAND
BIRDWATCHING ON MERSEYSIDE
THE LANCASTER CANAL
FIELD EXCURSIONS IN NW ENGLAND
ROCK CLIMBS LANCASHIRE & NW
THE ISLE OF MAN COASTAL PATH

DERBYSHIRE & EAST MIDLANDS
WHITE PEAK WALKS - 2 Vols
HIGH PEAK WALKS
WHITE PEAK WAY
KINDER LOG
THE VIKING WAY
THE DEVIL'S MILL (Novel)
WHISTLING CLOUGH (Novel)
WALES & WEST MIDLANDS
THE RIDGES OF SNOWDONIA
HILLWALKING IN SNOWDONIA
ASCENT OF SNOWDON
WELSH WINTER CLIMBS
SNOWDONIA WHITE WATER SEA & SURF
SCRAMBLES IN SNOWDONIA
ROCK CLIMBS IN WEST MIDLANDS
THE SHROPSHIRE HILLS A Walker's Guide

SOUTH & SOUTH WEST ENGLAND
WALKS IN KENT
THE WEALDWAY & VANGUARD WAY
SOUTH DOWNS WAY & DOWNS LINK
COTSWOLD WAY
WALKING ON DARTMOOR
SOUTH WEST WAY - 2 Vol

SCOTLAND
SCRAMBLES IN LOCHABER
SCRAMBLES IN SKYE
THE ISLAND OF RHUM
CAIRNGORMS WINTER CLIMBS
WINTER CLIMBS BEN NEVIS & GLENCOE
SCOTTISH RAILWAY WALKS
TORRIDON A Walker's Guide
SKI TOURING IN SCOTLAND

THE MOUNTAINS OF ENGLAND & WALES
VOL 1 WALES
VOL 2 ENGLAND

Also a full range of guidebooks to walking, scrambling, ice-climbing, rock climbing, and other adventurous pursuits in Europe

Other guides are constantly being added to the Cicerone List.
Available from bookshops, outdoor equipment shops or direct (send for price list)
from CICERONE, 2 POLICE SQUARE, MILNTHORPE, CUMBRIA, LA7 7PY

CICERONE GUIDES

Cicerone publish a wide range of reliable guides to walking and climbing in Europe

FRANCE
TOUR OF MONT BLANC
CHAMONIX MONT BLANC - A Walking Guide
TOUR OF THE OISANS: GR54
WALKING THE FRENCH ALPS: GR5
THE CORSICAN HIGH LEVEL ROUTE: GR20
THE WAY OF ST JAMES: GR65
THE PYRENEAN TRAIL: GR10
TOUR OF THE QUEYRAS
ROCK CLIMBS IN THE VERDON

FRANCE / SPAIN
WALKS AND CLIMBS IN THE PYRENEES
ROCK CLIMBS IN THE PYRENEES

SPAIN
WALKS & CLIMBS IN THE PICOS DE EUROPA
WALKING IN MALLORCA
BIRDWATCHING IN MALLORCA
COSTA BLANCA CLIMBS

FRANCE / SWITZERLAND
THE JURA - Walking the High Route and Winter Ski Traverses
CHAMONIX TO ZERMATT The Walker's Haute Route

SWITZERLAND
WALKS IN THE ENGADINE
THE VALAIS - A Walking Guide
THE ALPINE PASS ROUTE

GERMANY / AUSTRIA
THE KALKALPEN TRAVERSE
KLETTERSTEIG - Scrambles
WALKING IN THE BLACK FOREST
MOUNTAIN WALKING IN AUSTRIA
WALKING IN THE SALZKAMMERGUT
KING LUDWIG WAY

ITALY
ALTA VIA - High Level Walkis in the Dolomites
VIA FERRATA - Scrambles in the Dolomites
ITALIAN ROCK - Selected Rock Climbs in Northern Italy
CLASSIC CLIMBS IN THE DOLOMITES
WALKING IN THE DOLOMITES

OTHER AREAS
THE MOUNTAINS OF GREECE - A Walker's Guide
CRETE: Off the beaten track
Treks & Climbs in the mountains of RHUM & PETRA, JORDAN
THE ATLAS MOUNTAINS

GENERAL OUTDOOR BOOKS
LANDSCAPE PHOTOGRAPHY
FIRST AID FOR HILLWALKERS
MOUNTAIN WEATHER
MOUNTAINEERING LITERATURE
THE ADVENTURE ALTERNATIVE

CANOEING
SNOWDONIA WILD WATER, SEA & SURF
WILDWATER CANOEING
CANOEIST'S GUIDE TO THE NORTH EAST

CARTOON BOOKS
ON FOOT & FINGER
ON MORE FEET & FINGERS
LAUGHS ALONG THE PENNINE WAY

CICERONE

Also a full range of guidebooks to walking, scrambling, ice-climbing, rock climbing, and other adventurous pursuits in Britain and abroad

Other guides are constantly being added to the Cicerone List.
Available from bookshops, outdoor equipment shops or direct (send for price list)
from CICERONE, 2 POLICE SQUARE, MILNTHORPE, CUMBRIA, LA7 7PY

Printed by
Carnmor Print & Design, London Road, Preston